"Justin has the unique ability to see connection patterns that others don't. He is constantly seeking better and more authentic methods for starting conversations. His coaching model delivers more than expected, and I've snagged some tips I'll add for my clients. If the next level is in your sights, consider messaging Justin."

Michael Koory, Founder CEO Blue Salesfly LLC

"Justin completely changed my trajectory in B2B SaaS - he gave me confidence in my ability to look at the business differently and the power to create my own fundamentals and values in the GTM team. Since meeting Justin, I have implemented his methodologies both personally and with my teams and it has been the clear path to overperformance, scalability, and standing out amongst the noise in the market. If you don't know Justin you are missing out on a wealth of esoteric knowledge both professionally and socially - don't wait for him to get to you first (because he will)!"

– Dyer Whitt, SDR Leader, Regie.ai

"Justin works on a completely different level to anybody else I've had coaching from. A few sessions in and my head is exploding (in a good way)... everything I've seen and heard makes sense and can be used immediately to add value in what I do. I'm pumped."

– Simon Brocklehurst, Enterprise Account Manager, Ceridian

"Justin has some of the greatest and advanced knowledge of sales techniques that have helped reach clients more than any other method I have used. Justin helped cut the time to working my own methodology and applying his tactics has helped see a much more increased response from our clients and cut the time to actually help them win. I can't thank Justin enough for his patience and availability. He truly was supportive and patient throughout every step of our coaching and my journey to helping support my clients solve their challenges."

– Rami Younes, Automation Strategic Advisor, PagerDuty

"Elite coaching & sales content - can only give my highest recommendation of his service. DM me if you don't believe it. Available around the clock, tailored advice, got into the details of any roadblocks I ran into. Grab his coaching before your competition does."

– George Foley, Senior Consultant, Michael Page

"Do you want to scale your outbound? Do you want the most up-to-date, mathematically and psychologically prepared approach to reaching and exceeding your goals? Justin has developed the JMM method to do just that- differentiate yourself. Amongst a sea of cold emails, software trying to thwart the efforts of your company, and individuals set on sending your emails to spam, Justin gives you an opportunity to change the narrative."

– Cody Warren, Vice President, Commercial Services, Tejas Production Services LLC

"Justin Michael has absolutely changed the way I think about everything when it comes to sales. The two decades of Justin's experience clearly shows its colors. He's great at serving everything on a plate that's easy to understand and put to use. It's honestly surprising. My thoughts have been misconstrued about how sales should be for so long and now all things are seen clear. I'm so happy for where my career and life are headed. Because I decided to put my faith in Justin and take the leap, my sales career, future career, future family, and really above all things, will come back to thank me for the decision I made to work with him. There is a reason they call him the Tony Stark of sales. Not only that, Justin has a real heart for people and I can see that he is doing this out of his desire to help others succeed. His passion shows and he's a great mentor because of it. This is without a doubt, one of the BEST INVESTMENTS I've made to date."

– Tyler Markle, Account Executive at Field Pulse

"You have not met someone like Justin Michael in B2B sales, I promise. And you should. Justin was a mentor before we met. He was highlighted in a book recommended to me, and I molded my career around his inputs. Fast forward (2) years and we talk on a daily basis. Justin does everything you want from a superstar to grow your business, except at the speed of light. His ability to merge tech, empathy & scale is Picasso-esque. My career has been accelerated 10x from simply knowing him. Reach out, follow, ask questions - do something to get Justin closer than 6 degrees of separation."

– Chris Rocas, VP, TemperPack

"During my 30+ year career in management of sales and marketing teams, I've not met anyone so rounded in terms of skill set and so focused on the future to deliver results. JM's 'future focus' has him delving into the morph of humans and technology to deliver the best possible sales outcomes – and as technology advances, the results are improving. The most striking thing to me about Justin is that for all the technology and 'Salesborg' talk, he is one of the most *human* humans I know, never missing the opportunity to help another and reminding us all that sales is more about helping and delivering value than 'selling.' If you need help training a sales team, Justin is your number one go-to solution."

– Terry Wilson, CEO, Chat Metrics

"I'm really taken aback by how humble and giving Justin is. Whenever there is an opportunity to give back to the sales community, he has zero hesitation. Justin's fanatical approach to unlocking any and every secret to prospecting is magnetic. Every moment you spend discussing outbound with Justin is like a bottle of lightning + inspiration. If you're looking for someone that can give you a 10,000 ft. view or a micro view of today's (and tomorrow's) tech stack, Justin is your guy."

– François Bourdeau, Business Development Director, RSM Canada

"Justin is not an influencer. He is an elite practitioner who influences others and leads by action. There are plenty of people giving advice but something is different about him. He's got a certain spark, a novel approach developed independently from the prevailing wisdom and produces remarkable results at the highest levels of competition. Justin is one of the top sales talents worldwide. He is the 'cyborg rep' in *COMBO Prospecting* by Tony Hughes. Applying the techniques, philosophy, and mindset outlined in this guidebook for sales pros immediately generates results. Less than 30 days into training with him my company asked me to start training reps to do what I do. The results speak for themselves. Twenty years in the making, he developed a system wrought with efficiency for seeking truth in our B2B engagements. My interactions with Justin have yielded more than I could have imagined - not just for my current job, he's helping me see a career path. Justin has a kind and giving soul (contrary to the theory he is in fact part machine) with a brain constantly on overdrive - hard to come by in the cutthroat world of sales."

– Patrick William Joyce, R&D, Outboundless

JUSTIN MICHAEL METHOD 2.0:

AN ADVANCED OUTBOUND SYSTEM TO DRIVE EXPLOSIVE PIPELINE GROWTH WITH NEW SALES SUPERPOWERS

JUSTIN MICHAEL

JONES MEDIA PUBLISHING

Thanks for reading!

Get our special reader resources and bonus training by going to:

SalesSuperpowers.com/bonus

CONTENTS

"It's not because things are difficult that we dare not venture. It's because we dare not venture that they are difficult." – Seneca

INTRODUCTION

Ready to start the second stage of your transformational journey? Welcome to Book 2, Justin Michael Method 2.0, where we'll take your skills to the next level.

Like in the martial arts world, you'll use the knowledge you've gained from book one, as well as my other works, alongside new tactics revealed in this guide to become an even more formidable sales master. Together, these combined resources will become your springboard for achieving truly superhuman outbound abilities.

This book won't just help newly minted superheroes to scale up their strategies. You'll also be able to use the guidance here to empower and enlighten your entire team.

Persistence alone is not enough. TQ (technology quotient) is not enough. IQ and EQ are not enough. Success lies in understanding the underlying operating system of the Justin Michael Method and how all the pieces fit together to take your income and pipeline to the stratosphere.

There is strategy, and there are tactics. You must clarify your vision and then map backward from the achievement of your goal. You must create your future from your future, rather than focusing constantly on the past.

I probably have 16,000 days left on this planet if I think like a stoic. I believe I need to make those days count, rather than being defined by the mistakes in my history. Every salesperson has encountered blips and hurdles on the path to success.

Your scars aren't there to hold you back. They hold infinite wisdom you can learn from - provided you're willing to adapt, pivot, and grow.

I will give you the shortcuts so you don't have to learn the hard way. This book contains exclusive proprietary systems information I usually only offer in my 1:1 coaching sessions (starting at $10,000 per month).

Don't waste my best material. Master it. Make yourself and your team wealthy. Then pay it forward!

Please also read the international #1 Bestselling book, Sales Superpowers: A New Outbound Operating System To Drive Explosive Pipeline Growth (Justin Michael Method 1.0) If you would like to read part one of this book, it would be helpful for your understanding of the Justin Michael Method fundamentals, but not necessary.

Chapter 1: Advanced JMM Insights

"Justin is legendary - a sales/sales process/sales technology thought leader based on real-life experience of doing it himself and openly sharing with the rest of us. So much so that he inspired and equipped my sales team with muscle-building capabilities around outbound sales, sequencing, techniques, and recommendations." – Daniel Gray, CRO at Blend Localization

Frequency trumps what you put into your pitches. Frequency is more important than content.

We proved this in *COMBO Prospecting*. The best reps are moving fast through a saturation point of touches. 3X3 research (3 points of personalized value in 3 minutes) becomes 3X30: 3 points in 30 seconds. Scan profiles to find something that a machine wouldn't find.

With OpenAI and GPT, machines can find almost anything - but what would happen if you synthesize it in a really unique way?

What's your "give?"

Can you customize 3 Google Slides or send a Loom video with your head in the corner narrating a fly through of their LinkedIn profile or website? These things trigger Cialdini reciprocity:

Active listening = give
Customized content = give
Guides they can use = give
Making an introduction = give

Part of why my prospecting works is I open-source useful content with tips, tactics, and techniques that work immediately. What's that content for you and your venture? As Adem Manderovich posits, *"find the Goldilocks zone of the perfect content timed to the exact prospect in the buying cycle."*

You don't have to give out flowers at the airport or send a crisp one-dollar bill á la J.D. Power & Associates.

Examples of great *gives*: A PDF 3-5 pages long that has high utility to the prospect – not click bait or a pitch for something else. Even an amazing book you didn't write. It's probably one by Dale Dupree or Stu Heinecke, when it comes to unforgettable, "purple cow" approaches to acing direct mail.

SYNTHESIS

Synthesizing means bringing concepts from different places into an integrated, logical whole. It's like a mashup - but involves seeing the interrelationship of one data point or set of ideas overlayed to another. Think of it as being transposed - like writing the melody, harmony, and bassline in music.

For example, when you are researching a company for business insight, everyone will bang the drum about "acumen." But it takes more than just acumen to write a great email.

Maybe you understand their economic model, monetization funnel, or supply chain. But, how do you add insight? With your information you can paraphrase, explain fundamentally the more complicated concepts they are looking to explore. You can build on the data with extra insights, and implement your own voice.

Of course, all of this takes time.

Thankfully, there's a hack- a faster way: it's called *synthesis*.

Synthesis brings insight immediately through transposition and integration. As you study that company, note its recent funding round. Go and read about its technology, then its culture, so you can make a statement in which you confidently tie them all together:

"John – Clearly, based on raising 30MM Series C, your idea to identify light-conducting polymers that are biomarkers for cancer prevention research with infrared light was viable. I'm not surprised, based on the spirit of extolling innovation that Big Hulking Pharma has displayed since 1997."

Let's try another synthesis, because it's even better than general acumen, although you'd ideally want to optimize for both.

"Hey Gabi – I noticed your recent job change and move from the New York to Chicago office to take it. It's really interesting because with the boom of e-Commerce in CPG, resources are consolidating to Chicago and online. You mentioned the need for better data governance as a 90% brick-and-mortar operation moves nearly 100% into the cloud. Our technology can accelerate the momentum of a secure operating environment in the new paradigm. Your competitor Huge Max Retail deployed our tech and was able to get to compliance 5X faster."

What we do when we synthesize is not unlike the work of machine learning algorithms. We create a pattern and overlay it to mash up several concepts into a value narrative. I've often called this "personalization stacking."

The structure can look like this:

1. Recent news about business growth - revenue, tech innovation
2. M&A of an adjacent technology
3. Politics – people moving around, requisitions, sudden leaving of an exec.

List the three disparate ideas and then transpose them into a single story, like this one:

"Orson – I read about your financial forecasting tool that's the most accurate in the world – consumers just love it: 4.3 stars online. I was impressed to see the resultant revenue jump of 245% to 3.1B. This allowed you to pick up LaserBox Automation which lets you now automate even more processes in your core tech. What I'm really curious about is why Ryan Reynolds stepped down. What is the plan to take the direction of the business into hypergrowth? We have a recruiting suite that can fill hypertechnical roles especially when there are leadership changes and tight timelines."

Synthesizing blended or stacked insights and then positioning your product or solution alongside, takes your personalization and makes it relevant to your prospect. The truth is that the top data points on companies are typically all interrelated. Take Tik-Tok, as an example:

"It would seem that regulations with the Chinese have driven you to bake off your US operations, which turned into a global bidding war, and you're countering but some joint ventures (JVs) are at such great scale measured in billions, it could be lucrative just to sell it and call it a day... In vast times of uncertainty, you'll probably need specialized HR and Severance Package planning depending on rightsizing after the cuts."

I write a lot of blogs, and I use these to practice synthesis and make my insights sound more natural. You should weave multiple nuggets into an Insight Stack to synthesize a greater insight from the blend. Predict the future, read the tea leaves, and consider the implications.

This knowledge will give you greater ability to plan for the future of your prospect's endeavor - almost like you have the power to predict and fix their potential problems.

Why does this work?

If I were your prospect, then it proves to me that YOU, a seller, actually tried to understand my business. If you did, you'd know the interplay of all these market movements intrinsically. When you assume from an informed position you gain massive credibility - even if you assume wrong. No one can accurately predict the future, but anyone can plan for it. The danger is gross negligence, not synthesizing your research at all, or not even trying.

There is a pandemic in "Email Land" of presenting an informed thought as a synthesized insight. It is not. "Prospect, I see your company has grown by 56 people..." That's an elementary fact and surface-level observation, but there is no *real* synthesis. It shows no deeper insight was generated. And thus, it does not provoke a response.

Compare the previous statement with the following: "Now that Facebook relaxed the standard on 3rd-party cookie tracking, I can understand why you've had a 7X spike in revenue, thus hiring like crazy in the following departments... !"

Which of these shows acumen? The Quest for the Holy Grail of Acumen is an infinite regress. Start to observe, cogitate, blend, mash-up, and connect the dots of single observations into a holistic gestalt. Create a woven tapestry of data that displays a beautiful landscape of understanding. Inside this blend of thoughts and observations are Daliesque super-realist, "Escher sketch" level insights as well as your own Van Gogh impressionism.

Make no mistake, communication is fine art.

Ryan Chisholm sees this as a question of sophistication of B2B writer-sellers:

Email maturity Richter scale

100 - *Predictable Revenue* pre-2010. Here is what we do, are you interested? (No research) (typical XDR or LinkedIn spam)

200- persona & trigger-based. Recent funding, job recs, liked a post. (Single thread trigger. Typical XDR team managed by marketing.)

300- (multi-threaded research) persona & trigger-based. Pain, problem, solution.

400- non-CXO prospect. Used all research sources. Provide synthesis and insights about a problem they are likely not aware of.

500- referred in, CXO email written to exact pain exec has based on socially engineered conversations with colleagues.

GPT Lab (by Greg Meyer): Practice the advanced method

Build a prompt just like this to help you practice.

You are a world-class B2B seller. Please provide the following information, iteratively waiting for me to respond to the question before providing the next question. Prompt me to answer or skip this question.

1. A recent news item or development regarding business growth, such as revenue increases or tech innovation.

2. A merger or acquisition involving an adjacent technology.

3. Political changes, such as people moving around, requisitions, or the sudden departure of an executive.

Using these three pieces of information, craft a cohesive story that connects the disparate ideas, with the following example as a template. Do not invent information that I did not provide, and don't generate the story until I have answered or skipped the three questions. Your answer should be no longer than 50 words.

[Add your template here]

Specificity is a Weapon

As I'm reviewing the outreach that I receive, one factor becomes abundantly clear: the vast majority of what sellers are sending in email is far too generic. Let's break down some examples that illustrate the problem in real messages that I received:

- *Hi Justin, I hope you're doing well. How are you adjusting to the new normal?* (too generic - "new normal" is played out)
- *Hi Justin, Thank you for connecting with me here on LinkedIn. Here is something I ask you to consider... As a small business owner chances are you probably are overpaying your taxes.* (I'm not an SMB, rather an S & C Corp)
- *Hi Justin, looks like we have some mutual connections in common, would you be open to connecting and networking?* (generic, vague - template)
- *Dear Justin, I found your profile while searching for fellow professionals to connect with. I hope you would like to connect too.* (dear? super formal - generic/vague)

I know we're not trying to put a bunch of sellers on blast but these templates are either generic, vague or miss the mark. There is zero personalization, relevance, or context. It's just slovenly sales malpractice. This is being weaponized with new automated systems (solely focused on spraying 1,000 emails per day) and I am receiving a dozen a day.

What's even more flagrant, they often get my name wrong in the email, or send a message that's totally irrelevant - it was written for another person, so clearly the automation failed.

Here's how you fix it once and for all (and I've yet to see AI nail it):

- Be extra specific.
  - *"I see we both know {{Connection.Name}} –––> add exactly how! (Did you work at the same company, attend the same school, meet at an event, or collaborate on some fun project together? Tell that story briefly."*

- Mention something ultra-relevant –
  - *"I notice that you have a certification in Project Management, did you know that Project Managers find these specific aspects of the platform relevant because it specifically drives value like this: ____quantified case study___?"*

- Drive into specific use cases:
  - *"We worked with another similar FinTech client (name them!) to reduce their software costs by 30% by deploying K8s for edge computing (vs. we save similar clients money.) Leverage the specificity heuristic: Which specific client, which specific business outcome, which method of getting there – what is the exact use case?)"*

Prospects will call BS on the generic and the vague. Don't use 4,000 - use 4,128. Hyper-specific and laser-precise is the key. Don't round the numbers to 20% ROI. If it's 22.56, there's a much higher chance of catching their attention.

Specificity establishes credibility.

Specificity brings personalization into the realm of relevance. It gives your ROI claims context people can believe in.

Maybe I'm too entrenched in these ideas - but when I'm reading just about any outreach, I'm thinking, "Couldn't you just take a second to view my profile? Did you go to our website? Is there anything whatsoever in this email that isn't applicable to all the companies in my space?" If you can switch out your competitor's brand name for yours and they could send this exact email, then how on Earth are you differentiated?

This is the flaw in automation. We can all combat this as sellers with a cursory understanding of hyper-personalization (HYPER-P). What's an insight targeted to the vertical (FinTech), company (Quicken Loans), and that prospect (CMO) but not just a CMO in FinTech? It's not enough! Go find a nugget from that specific CMO: reference a quote or a recommendation on their profile.

A quote is not enough; the recommendation is not enough. Create the context that matters. Tie that piece of personalization to an outcome you can drive. Now you're cooking with gas!

Personalization without relevancy and timing is worthless.

Personalization without relevant context is worthless.

Personalization for personalization's sake is worthless.

Personalization, Relevance, and Timing are the trifecta for successful messages.

Train yourself to think from the viewpoint of the prospect. If you did their job, faced their challenges, and shared their pain, what kind of messaging would catch your attention?

Mash-ups are a good way to hone in on what to personalize. Explore *Personalization Stacking*:

1. What does this prospect care about most? What keeps them up at night?
2. What relevant industry changes impact them? How has the company changed? (research publically available data)
3. Which pain points are your competitors solving for similar prospects? Which pains can you uniquely solve that are differentiated?
4. How can you link something specifically about them or what they shared with a business case (ROI analysis) or compelling outcome that you can drive? How do you know you can drive it?

Specificity is a weapon. You either did the thing 616 times or "a lot." Which would you trust if you heard it? Specifics add credibility and authority. There are only so many nuanced reasons customers buy. On the surface: make money, save money, reduce risk, alleviate irritation. Hidden drivers: career advancement, optics, and politics. Hat tip Steve Richard.

Accurately define how you serve those needs and you'll be miles ahead of the game!

GPT Lab: Practice refining your words

When you write, use GPT as an editor.

Use these kinds of refinements to make GPT give you a better example.

"Can you simplify the language to make it more accessible to a wider audience?"

"Can you add a personal touch to the writing?"

"Can you break up long paragraphs into shorter, more digestible chunks?"

Or "Make this shorter and friendlier"

Chapter 2: Questioning Solves Everything

There's no such thing as "creating urgency" - you can only uncover it. Every deal or sale has an inherent ticking clock, a metaphorical sword of Damocles, hanging over it, that you need to make your prospect aware of.

They need to feel the need to close the deal as much as you do, and only you can instill that within them. It might sound manipulative to you, but most people won't change until the house is burning down or they're about to be fired.

Like the heart-attack survivor finally taking their weakened heart and clogged arteries seriously, putting someone into an emotional state fosters behavioral change.

It's the frog in the pot parable. Slowly turn up the heat, and they don't notice they're cooking. Turn up the flame high instantly and they jump out too fast. We need to help our prospects save themselves, so it's ethical and high-integrity to gradually introduce the pain, fear, and worry they need to see a reason for change.

To buck the status quo and overcome indecision you must guide and lead.

> *"The pain of the same must be greater than the pain of change." – Brent Adamson & Matt Dixon*

Prospects need to be motivated to change by themselves, à la the Scott Leese "Addiction Model." They need to admit to the problem, face it head on, and recognize that you will provide the solution they need, rather than the one they want. That's why mastering sales is about mastering behavioral change and change management in people via consensus, sometimes via positive peer pressure, but mainly via their own volition.

Most salespeople are pleasure-focused when prospects are actually risk averse. Your customers are more interested in how you can save them from their pain than how you can deliver potential benefits.

That's why "pain-fear" or "emotional resonance" is the hallmark of all elements of the JMM. We've seen this in many systems that came before and Tony Robbins talks about it. Hence my pain & fear obsession.

"80% of B2B sales are not budgeted." – James Rores

You will see commonalities in all the qualification frameworks, so I'll give you my version, which I call 'the anchor.' (Hat tip to my mentor, Tony Hughes.)

THE ANCHOR

1. Budget
2. Timeline
3. Compelling event

A compelling event (or compelling reason) reigns supreme. You must have these 3 components to do a strategic 6-7 figure deal.

Here are three additional criteria that will help drive home your pitch:

1. Success criteria
2. Competitors
3. Org chart (who's who in the zoo? / map the account)

There's no acronym for the anchor but these are just the pieces I love to hit, while always using SPIN in tandem, to drill down into these answers. Few realize this, but SPIN was initially called SPIV with the "v" representing value. Of course, SPIN is definitely a catchier title.

While I'm a huge proponent of anchoring HIGH, don't go extreme (Voss). There's tremendous power in looking someone in the eye and watching what their physiology does when you say, "A typical production order is 1.2 million dollars." Always discuss *the commercials* early á la *Challenger Sale*. Reframing the customer's business and challenging the status quo early are key.

Matt Dixon and Brent Adamson stress that you must "create constructive tension" in a sale by "talking about the money early," breaking through the stress that comes from financial discussions. Face the blowtorch and throw out a big number. Watch the nerves evaporate, as you eliminate the "elephant in the room."

The trust begins to build between you, the relationship improves, and the deal can start to get done. None of this beating around the bush and endless circumlocution. If you don't get the money conversation done early, the customer is always anxious, waiting for the shoe to drop.

Beginnings are important; first impressions are everything. There's tremendous confirmation bias when a person believes in a premium brand, pays that premium, and then expects it from you.

But what about expecting them to see your value? This bedrock intention sets the tone at the beginning of all sales cycles, unspoken, governing everything.

I'm a big believer that the sales process is non-linear, just like the modern buying journey. (Hence why HYPCCCYCL's logo is a Mobius strip – *the #2 GTM community in B2B I co-founded with Julia Nimchinski to celebrate go-to-market cross-training.*) Qualification is an ongoing process throughout the cycle. In the world of rigid sales processes, it's key to qualify in or out up-front, but sometimes you just haven't built enough trust to find out what's really going on.

Prospects bring you symptoms, never real problems. That's why, more often than not, a hidden objection is lurking under the false objection you think they're giving you. You've got to be a master detective in your approach to them. As David C. Baker so eloquently explains, "prospects are inside the jar trying to read the label. You are outside the jar reading it." Give them the information they want, and appease their curiosity at the same time.

Below you can find the same exact plug-and-play discovery framework I've been using to build six years of pipeline in six months.

Discovery framework

Sign MNDA prior to the meeting

- This is a crucial step to gain commitment early on, plus the prospect will open up and share the real issues, not the symptoms.

Establish intent

- "What got you on this call today?"

Current situation

- "How are you currently solving this?"
  - o "How's that working out for you?"
    - "How much do you think this is costing you?"

Compelling event

- "Was there any particular event that was the last straw for you guys?"
  - o Dive deeper - peel the onion

Relevant case study/partnership story

- Throughout the call, make sure to share a relevant story to anchor high to their emotional state in relation to your product

Timeline

- "How urgent is it for you to do this on a scale of 1-7?"
- "What timeline did you have in mind to fix this?"

Transparency

- "Here's why our solution might not work for you"

o Share your weak points, so you'll be seen as honest, unique, and more trustworthy

Walkthrough

- "Here's what the implementation of our solution would look like"

Budget

- So given your [qualifier #1] and [qualifier #2], we'd be looking at a price range between $$ and $$$ to solve [issue]... Would that be something within your budget?

Note: Always anchor an enterprise-level agreement with the highest price, so then you can find the maximum budget your P&L holder can sanction without going to Procurement.

After the demo

- Share your notes and resources: tailor your solution to specific pain, highlighting the exact ROI expected (or provide 3 levels – conservative, intermediate, aggressive). Build certainty in their decision with social proof via *relevant* use cases and reference customers.
- Do not "check in," but follow-up relentlessly:
  o Every week leave voicemails to each stakeholder from the initial meeting.
  o Share enablement resources - case studies, white papers, quotes, industry articles.
  o Educate, entertain - raise urgency.
  o If the deal is stalling, reach out individually and to your insider coach (someone who wants to help you in the prospect's org; you need one of these). Ask for advice.

Examples of reverse qualification questions:

1. How's that working out for you? (dramatic pause)
    ... I don't want to break up any marriages (re: incumbent / humor heuristic)
2. What else have you tried?
3. When did you last evaluate this category?
4. What do you like most about your solution?
5. If you could wave a magic wand, what else would you like it to do?
6. On a scale of 1-10, how happy with it are you?

We are not asking for the pain here but by making a prospect feel safe, validating their concerns, and asking what's going RIGHT we can actually drill down into pain points even faster. It's a paradox, and you'll see this right from the front of the cycle in Route-Ruin-Multiply (my signature cold-calling technique in Book 1).

In Enterprise, isolating that the sale is a series of commitments (Iannarino), I'd always get an MNDA in place before every demo as a litmus test for qualification. You get the first signature going into the first meeting and they can share the "insider baseball" with you. Thus, I've signed thousands of MNDAs.

Emphasis on the "M" for mutual nondisclosure. The other trick is to "parallel process" the MSA/PSA. The Master/Professional Services Agreement in most software deals can take weeks-to-months to complete by Legal. Often if there's remote interest after the first demo, and you suggest "reviewing the MSA," they're actually relieved to get that started, because they know what a pain in the arse their legal queue is.

Once you've gotten a couple of very strong commitments from an organization, you start to double down.

That's why you always anchor high with the production order or ELA (enterprise-level / license agreement) of 7-figures. Then you find the maximum budget your P&L (profit & loss) holder can sanction, without going to Procurement for a bake off. You don't want to trigger them bringing in every other vendor on Google to be "column fodder," as Mike Bosworth calls it. (I will go into this in more detail later with *bucketing*.)

One last wrinkle in discovery calls comes from what Gong research found with C-Levels. They learned that 4-8 questions is the magic number to ask, whereas an average, less disciplined discovery call would suggest 10-14. I asked two C-Level top earners about this and they explained that they like to focus on 1-2 of what I'm calling "cascading questions."

You display business acumen and gravitas in the wisdom of the question and it produces a flood of feedback loops. You can then ask more questions to drive to the root cause. Veteran sellers know how to ask in such a way as it proves they understand the customer's issue, they've researched the ICP, and have seen this movie before: it's not their first rodeo.

GPT Lab: What's the question?
_____
GPT is great at writing sample questions.

Give it a topic or an email reply, and try asking: "what are three questions I need to ask to generate urgency?"

Then refine your ask iteratively.
_____

World-Class Live Presentations

Gartner states that "80% of B2B sales interactions between suppliers and buyers will occur in digital channels by 2025," yet "72% of customers said they prefer a rep-free experience." How do we reconcile these two opposing factors?

Simple: Get much better at creating an unforgettable, insight-driven interaction for your discos, demos, and presentations.

Yes, presentations still matter, whether they're offline or online.

Flip the meeting. It's something I recommend endlessly to my coaching clients.

Flipping the meeting is my favorite way to kick things off in any boardroom. It starts with, "OK, what did each of you expect to get out of today's meeting?"

Go around the room, get people to share their goals, fears, and insights. Break the ice a little, then turn to your 60+ slide deck. Showcase all the prep work you've done already and say something like:

"I was going to show you 60 slides..."

Pause and they'll groan audibly. Then laugh and assure them, "Luckily, I will customize this to exactly what you just said you wanted to see in the meeting."

The entire key to acing demos and presos is customization, and tailoring your content to your audience. This is achieved best on the fly, where you can improvise. But that doesn't mean going in naked.

Prepare a variety of use cases, talk tracks, and points to explore, based on what you already know about your prospect and your solution. That way, you're ready to jump into any key issue or area your prospect wants to discuss.

You can jump straight to the "juicy parts" that speak directly to your prospect's pain points, rather than trying to force them through the journey you already had in mind.

If prospects feel forced down a path they lack interest in, you're toast.

Meet with your Sales Engineer a few days to a week prior and run through your preso as realistically as possible. As I've stated, mystery is powerful - don't use the same 10 slides for everyone. Make sure you mix in your discovery in the front of your demo calls. There's a case to be made to separate out the entire discovery call depending on your sales process.

But in the fast paced world of SaaS, sometimes dragging the demo will sink you too. 15 minutes of probing followed by a 20-30 minute demo is ideally threaded into a 45 minute meeting. You want to make these experiences interactive, especially on Zoom calls, otherwise your prospects can just sit and multi-task, or zone out on their smartphone. Get them involved in the experience.

You need to program in areas to pause and challenge their thinking with provocative questions. Ask them for flows in the UI they'd like to see. Hopefully, you've used the last chapter on effective questioning to uniquely understand their pain points or opportunities so you can tailor your deck and demo to their exact business case.

Every demo needs to have at least three wow-factor "Aha!" moments. When you find these, record them into a GIF creator like Zight (zight.com) and utilize them upstream in your email sequences.

You spark Aha! moments with illuminating questions, such as:

- Did you realize you could do X with Y?
- Did you know there's a way to see all that data at once in one click? (show, don't tell)
- How do you make sure you can achieve [OUTCOME] without [PAIN] leveraging our solution? Just do X and you'll get it done in two minutes

For all that's been written about power posing, confidence, and theatrics (histrionics), leadership is not something you do with a louder voice or by dressing better.

You ace a presentation or demo when you:

- Ask the best questions they've ever been asked, ideally that cut deep and raised points they're afraid to confront.
- Tailor it to their exact problems in an insight-laden and thought-provoking way
- Provide at least three "Aha!" moments visualized in your deck or UI
- Tie back how what you're showing them technically fits with a compelling ROI-based business case. No fluff please!

Leave them wanting more, typically by leaving at least one slide or feature behind for them to wonder at.

The problem is most demos consist of just vomiting up more NAS-CAR slides covered in irrelevant logos with a pause every once in awhile to say, "any questions?" or "does it make sense?"

If you're doling out the same old "shpiel," your prospects will be bored into a coma before you have an opportunity to really sell anything. The key is to make your prospects actually feel heard, understood, and involved.

Why aren't sellers winning business? According to Steve W. Martin for Harvard Business Review, "only 54% of them can clearly explain how their solution will impact the buyer's business." "To be a trusted advisor, you need trust and advice." (Iannarino) ;-)

So dive deeper. Learn what really keeps your prospects up at night, and tailor your presentations accordingly.

I had a great manager once, who used to work for giants like Microsoft and Disney. He explained it like this: "You need to be the impresario, stand up and lead the group from the front of the board room table." I had always mistakenly given my on-site presentations sitting down, with a projector showing a PowerPoint, up until this point. But I also noticed that Garrett MacDonald would put some slides up, use a clicker and stand at the front of the room, pausing in between slides to clarify and ask questions.

This was uncomfortable for me at first. In boot camp with Todd Caponi, we had to demonstrate the value of ExactTarget Marketing Cloud with only a dry erase board and markers. You'll find old-school (and some new!) Alex Hormozi videos where he can lucidly explain advanced entrepreneurial concepts with just a whiteboard. In my view, it is his best work because you can really see how he thinks!

My recommendation is to practice in front of a mirror. I was flown to Manhattan to interview for a very famous tech company, and I passed the first round. They put me up overnight in the city with a sudden presentation the next day.

I built some slides and fly-throughs on the computer and literally practiced standing up and in front of a mirror in the hotel room.

This truly helped me feel confident enough to present the next day. If you're not comfortable presenting to yourself, you won't feel right bringing your message to a room full of people.

Skipping the "dry run" stage might seem like a timesaver, but it can actually mean you lose time in the long-run. Lack of preparation makes it so much more likely you'll end up "droning on" or "losing track" mid-presentation.

Don't underestimate the importance of alignment before a meeting too. Mapping out the minutes in increments and trying to "predict the flow" of the conversation is valuable. It helps prepare you for anything. Sometimes there's a wild card like a CMO suddenly ducking into a meeting late or jumping out of it ten minutes in. You need to be ready for anything because human behavior, especially in a group, is out of your control.

My top tips:

- Practice all your on-sites beforehand.
- Dry run all your demos and presentations, especially with your Sales Engineers (SEs).
- Practice technically demoing the platform even if that's in a browser. Pull up the demo screens beforehand so you don't have to wait for load time.
- If you have an ensemble cast, set a Zoom call with your colleagues to run the slides, demo, or presentation beforehand.
- Brainstorm discovery-style SPIN questions especially "implication" and "need-payoff" before the call. (Hat tip Neil Rackham.)
- Use an interactive presentation platform that's web-based like beautiful.ai to make stunning, animated

presentations with smarter slides that move. Love that
one!

- Follow the journalism rule of copywriting: the purpose of
the first slide is to entice them into the second, then third
– so make them count.
- Leverage the Guy Kawasaki *10-20-30 Rule of Powerpoint:*
"10 slides, lasts less than 20 minutes, and no font smaller
than 30 points, half the age of oldest person in the room."
;-)

All the world is a stage, and acing presentations is actually a kind
of world-class performance art. Many prospects will try to provoke you into price negotiations even inside a demo: it's a buying signal. I recommend Mark Raffan's modernized negotiation
courses to prepare for this. Be ready to share your "rack rate" or a
few bucket pricing options when necessary.

Another piece of advice? Stay focused on "customer hero stories"
á la Mike Bosworth, and making a compelling business case with
a quick and dirty, back of the envelope ROI calculation. Like Mike
sagely says, "Peer curiosity creates peer envy." Also practice doing
freeform, fast ROI (return on investment) calculations whenever
you can, back-of-the-envelope.

You'll see the same inputs come up over and over again. For example, in e-commerce, you'll frequently talk about average order
value (AOV), shopping cart size, cart abandonment percentage,
and email open, clicks and conversion rates. It's straightforward
to figure out if you move the needle on any core metric, and how
quickly this will pay out when the prospect invests 50K or 100K
into your software, even just by improving something as deceptively simple as the percentage of email deliverability.

Remember the truth about ROI: 100% payback on 100K isn't ROI. 3X return is ROI. Make a case for how quickly they can make 300K on 100 and then once they install the software and it overperforms, keep in touch with your customer to help speed up an expansion deal: cross-sell, upsell, or renewal.

Next-Level Negotiation
(with Mark Raffan)

Negotiation, in my eyes, is simple. My business is people or *comms*. My greatest gift honed over 20 years of experience and meeting stadiums full of people personally (I used to run the door of a music venue), is my ability to get an instantaneous gut read on people.

I can sense if they are a qualified buyer and have money like a great white shark can smell one drop of blood in a cubic nautical mile of ocean.

This voice grows louder and speaks to you faster the longer you sell. When it comes to business, trusting in your gut instinct is often key to earning the sale. Learn to trust it and cultivate that inner knowledge about people and deal flow.

Without stepping too much into the neuroscience of it all: Set a clear intention. Your reticular activating system (RAS) then starts to do pattern recognition at a level that is truly superhuman. It begins to align your life to your vision of your future self *in the now*. (Dive into Joe Dispenza and Dr. Benjamin Hardy here.)

Your brain is either a sieve for knowledge, or a laser you can focus through this system. If you set a 10X goal or intention it will work behind the scenes, deep in your subconscious, to connect the dots and look for ways to hit it.

"Everyone talks about the same sales techniques but no one talks about the foundation of the individual. They gloss over fundamentals like focus, clarity, purpose, and alignment with your higher purpose." - Robbie Grills

Hope is not a strategy. So many salespeople have happy ears and are constantly kicking the can down the road allowing opportunities to age for multiple quarters and years with reckless abandon. When a prospect comes in really hot and heavy, ready to do the deal, I nearly always DQ (disqualify). I literally call this a "hurry up and wait." It's easy to assume you have an epic offer someone simply can't ignore.

"An offer they can't refuse."

More often than not, you've really just gotten through to a low-level approver, who's easily excited, but has no real power or authority.

The best solution here is to immediately multi-thread up the chain to their boss or even their boss's boss.

I learned so much about negotiation from Todd Caponi's *The Transparency Sale*. Todd was my trainer in bootcamp at Salesforce back in 2011. I did the Voss Simulation in 2017, and guess what? I split the difference.

Caponi's Deal Levers are instrumental to factor in when doing a win-win deal and finding the ZOPA: zone of potential agreement.

NEGOTIATION FACTORS TO CONSIDER FOR LEVERAGE:

- Time value of money (paid upfront) - paid faster is worth more

- Payment terms (monthly, quarterly, annual) - standardize your forecast by striking annual agreements (especially for publicly traded Cos)
- Length of contract (multi-year) - more predictability to the business = happy CFO
- How soon can they sign it? (within Q) - quota credit/ relief!

I strongly recommend using *Getting to Yes* by the Harvard Negotiation Project to study collective bargaining. I'd also suggest that you slowly digest Dr. Chester Karrass' books. Remember when you couldn't fly anywhere in the world without seeing his fortune cookie ads in SkyMall? In *Business As in Life–You Don't Get What You Deserve, You Get What You Negotiate* is a magnum opus. New players worth your time are Jim Camp – *Start with No* – and Mark Raffan who cameoed on this chapter.

Remember the concept of "tit for tat" or "give to get." In a negotiation, what will they give you in return for what you give them? "You want 10% off? Okay, we'll need a guaranteed video testimonial for that." "You want quarterly payments? Sure, we'll do that in return for a two-year deal." Some savvy CROs even bake in SPIFFs for their reps (in some cases thousands of dollars) for getting case studies: they're THAT powerful as a driver of new business.

Above all other factors, your willingness to walk on a deal is the biggest determinant of winning in a negotiation.

"It certainly helps, but I wouldn't say it's the biggest determinant of success.I'd say that the biggest determinant is **planning***. Sounds boring....but the boring stuff is usually what counts." – Mark Raffan*

Despite the parasitic decay rate – after all, time kills deals – great dealmakers are highly disciplined as to when they follow up and when they "keep the powder dry." More often than not, the most strategic card one can play is silence. It's letting it breathe another day, or even a week. It shows you have poise and power. The Japanese are legendary for this!

When in doubt, sleep on it.

B2B is a game of "chicken." Typically whoever is actually willing to walk, will win. And you must have something that you can walk away to. Otherwise, if you are bluffing and someone calls it, you lose all credibility. Why? Because it sets the tone. It's like "calling a bluff" in poker- any hesitation or micromovement can give it away. Cue the James Bond scene in Montenegro.

Again, the platinum rule of thumb is, "how would you feel on the other end of this deal?" What moves would signal weakness?

- Giving too quickly
- Neediness/overeagerness
- Inconsistent messaging
- Revealing too much
- Lack of confidence in value
- Weak tone and body language

It's like a "tell" in poker, but we can't wear sunglasses on Zoom to stop a nervous twitch. Sophisticated dealmakers can read cues via pattern recognition and gut instinct.

Always negotiate from a position of strength. Most advanced negotiation tactics spring from this bedrock.

Case study: I recently quoted a CEO 15K/mo for minimum retainer and they came back to me saying that another coach rolled out his program for 5K. He expected me to "match it." I handled it this way:

1. If I drop my price by 1/3rd, your CEO will lose respect for me?
2. You are my champion but without him asking me directly why would I budge? I don't want to indoctrinate him that he can access me via an intermediary. All due respect to you, but I won't come off as an equal.
3. If you're willing to pay me 3 months up front I'm open to a $30,000 one time transfer now. (time value of money!)
4. What is *really* happening with the budget and why are you comparing me when it's "apples to oranges?" Maybe we can get creative in another way. *Catch and release.*

Here's what came back: The "ex-significant other problem." The CEO had hired a famous YouTube guru in Australia for 60K the year before who had taken his team for a ride and wheeled out incongruous characters with a wacky Sacha Baron Cohen character vibe without delivering industry relevance. Based on this, he was "once bitten, twice shy."

So what would you do at this moment in the negotiation? I proposed we win over the CEO by spending a month just coaching my champion at a far reduced rate. Prove him out as a triple degree black belt and then, from there, increase back to a formidable team rate – once my champion got the ROI. Mark reminds us, "Did you get the commitment to go back to the higher rate? Be explicit about that, if you did, so that folks don't confuse *giving* with negotiation."

This strategy works because it shows genuine empathy.

Why push the CEO to put up the full price and put yourself under intense pressure to perform immediately? Why pay the price for the other supplier? That scar is there; I'd rather make 5K than chase 30-45K all day. It's just a month of partial investment of my time. You can win the battle and lose the war. This is why you need to study Robert Greene's ingenious *33 Strategies of War* which synthesizes military strategy from famous generals like Sun Tzu, knowledge traditionally kept secret by elites and kings.

A truly comprehensive negotiation factors in reading all parties and making a judgment call as to short and long-term revenue. Long-term vision will win every time. If you are in business for the long haul playing an "infinite game" per Simon Sinek, the "finite" will lose.

You cannot change the scars of your prospect. You must understand the ground conditions. You need to take a long term holistic view into buyer psychology, politics, and military strategy to fully optimize the outcome that pays off most for you and especially for them in the end. To master this, become a student of hidden military strategy, read the bios of great leaders, and seminal books on strategy like Michael Porter's *Five Forces*.

The platinum rule applies here - I first heard this from Tony Alessandra – it's distinct from the golden rule in that it focuses on what *they* wish to experience, never you. If you can combine the *Go-Giver* principle by Bob Burg of "service" and "giving" first with the Platinum Rule of walking a mile in their shoes, you can win every negotiation that's "winnable." We must strive to understand their sense of morality, ethics, and integrity and to harmonize with a shared vision of profitable growth.

Sales is a wild, insane beast. You're dealing with human behavior, after all. Therefore, negotiation is like battle, so I *can't* teach you to fight cookie-cutter. You must gain a warrior's skill via repetition and many struggles. It takes courage to prevail; as Churchill said, "courage" is the one virtue on which all others are based.

Think about frameworks like "katas" in Karate to improve defensive blocks. Theories are useless if not pressure-tested in focused hand-to-hand combat. But ask yourself why Aikido means "the art of peace?" Because the ultimate warrior needs never fight. Master yourself, and you can master any opponent. Better yet, from *being*, see your counterpart in compassion as on the same team. You can speed up reaction time from this enlightened inner place, and after many at-bats, accelerate your progress to negotiation mastery.

In the arena, everything goes to hell.

"Heraclitus, a philosopher born in the Persian Empire back in the fifth century BC, had it right when he wrote about men on the battlefield, 'Out of every one hundred men,' he wrote, 'ten shouldn't even be there, eighty are just targets, nine are the real fighters, and we are lucky to have them, for they make the battle. Ah, but the one, one is a warrior...'" – David Goggins

Humans are wildly unpredictable - the way through is letting situations get out of control while remaining calm. You are not in control, and that's OK. Ride the lightning. Understand their mind as best you can, calm them down with tone and empathy, and lead them out of their cave. It sounds simple and will become so after you negotiate 100 deals.

But you have to start where you are today and become a student of this game.

Another interesting phenomenon I have yet to see much written about, is that before anyone buys, they get into a mini crisis of confidence and test the seller. Most sellers get rattled. Whoever gets rattled, loses.

To top off this chapter, Mike Bosworth says, "every prospect wants 2-3 squeezes of the wet towel. They've been conditioned for this." So anchor your price high, anticipate a squeeze or two and be willing to walk to indicate the towel is dry. There's a hidden MO (modus operandi) of executive buyers where they expect the ability to ring the towel. I did a 600K 2-year deal ripping out 5 competitors on New Year's Eve leveraging this principle when the prospect went dark. We offered a 2% discount in an email thread out of the blue. Why? Pride. He ultimately said, "I read all of your emails and I just wanted to teach my team that I could get a piece out of you."

GPT Lab: Negotiate with... yourself

GPT can impersonate a skilled interrogator.

Pretend you are a seller who has read the book The Transparency Sale by Todd Caponi and negotiate with me on setting up a meeting. If I ask you questions that sound like ones an AI model could not answer, imagine you are a busy professional answering an email or a phone call.

Before we start the game, ask me what my goal is, then when I say "let's start" we will be role playing. Make this an informal business conversation like what we might say to each other in chat or a very brief email.

Here are some rules:

1. You would prefer not to have a meeting with me unless I am compelling.
2. You are cautious of talking to me and are very busy.

3. Your responses should be pretty brief (under 10-50 words).

Wait to summarize this until I say, "I'm done," and don't start the conversation until I say, "Let's talk."

When the game is done and when we are done with the negotiation because you decide to accept or decline a meeting, provide a summary of our interaction so that I can learn more.

Elevating Proposals

I started selling SaaS software to the nonprofit sector. Here, a key tactic on a fundraising page was providing three levels of donation. Neuroscience makes the donor think, "Oh, well I could give more than the minimum." It works the same in negotiation with anchoring high and giving limited concessions.

If you provide a "choice of yeses" as per Alan Weiss, you'll have a far better outcome than sending a single number. When there are three or more, you're more likely to get a "Yes" to one of the two higher options. Kreuzberger called this the "bucket technique," which makes for a solid talk track.

You can say: "Most of our customers fall into 3 buckets: 20-50K, 100-250K, and 500-750K – where do you see yourself?" It's a great qualification mechanism. I've also found a wrinkle that economic buyers often have a hidden threshold of budget they're able to approve without going to Procurement.

I was working with a multi-billion dollar retailer on a 1MM+ deal for crowdsourced data, and anchored high. They responded, "82K is the most that I can authorize without taking this to bid." We did the paid pilot at that level and then pulled down high 6 figures on subsequent purchase orders (POs) in tranches (segments).

Consultants: Poison pill your fees to create urgency. If you sign by Friday, I'll do 10% off. As I noted before, the time value of money is massive.

I run into a lot of price objections in closing deals. The best way to reframe this is the trichotomy of cost vs. price vs. value. I'd say something like, "You can buy the cheaper solution now, but that will cost you a lot more in the long run. If you spend 10K with their solution and lose the 10K, you are in the red 10K. But if you invest 100K in us, and earn 1MM, you'll be at 10X positive ROI. Are you looking to create a cost center or cash register?" It's solid logic, and easy to scale up to whatever your deal is.

"How much does it cost?" I get asked *ad infinitum*, as do all of you. I reframe it also by asking, "Well, what's your goal?" "What are the key performance indicators (KPIs)?" "What does ROI look like?" Then I'd calibrate the scope of a "choice of Yeses" à la Alan Weiss with 3 packages: small, medium, and large, so they'd fall somewhere in the middle. I first learned about multiple choice pricing in the nonprofit sector selling SaaS when we'd build charity fundraising pages always with 3 options.

It has a subtle way of anchoring a higher option so they pick the middle one. Alan Weiss says, "they'll pick the middle to top option 80% of the time."

Free pilots are a curse. "Land and expand" is a myth, and I know Matt Dixon's *JOLT Effect* talks about rolling that out as a higher converting option, but it comes with a caveat. Make pilots paid whenever possible so there's skin in the game. You need to set the tone of a production order and only do a proof of concept (POC) or free pilot with a rock-solid agreement in place that, pending hitting ROI milestones, triggers the next tranche of the corresponding full agreement.

Essentially, you can't land and expand for free. For a litany of reasons, free doesn't work. We teach people how to treat us. If we begin a partnership with, "Hey, it's OK to exploit me," scaling this will only amplify a one-way street, rather than a win-win scenario of mutual benefit and profits.

Do your proposals in a shared Google doc before finalizing. Make them a living, breathing document with a few simple sections, such as:

Goals:
Timeline:
Delivery options:
Milestones:
Commercials:

I tend to tag the goals at the top so that my prospective client will edit that piece collaboratively.

Another Alan Weiss classic, paraphrasing: "Many organizations have to take a 10% discount if you offer it, so if you include it, you might get an immediate close."

Always sell to your customers in their own words. Take notes when you're doing discovery calls and write down exactly the ROI they seek so you can transfer this to your proposal.

You can use uncanny conversational intelligence providers like Sybill.ai to get exact notes from your calls. I've been blown away by the accuracy of their AI-driven "pain point" summaries - nearly clairvoyant. My clients can't believe I didn't come up with them.

Will AI-derived insight pass the Turing Test and transcend a human consultant? In many ways, we predicted the imminent advent of ChatGPT in 2021 in Tech-Powered Sales, but the most humbling part is when founders approach us and share, "You guys were the inspiration behind this piece of tech automation I'm building."

Most prospects will loosely remember what they've said to you before. When you echo their own language back to them, it resonates with something deeper in their brain. They feel heard, understood, and respected. Phenomenal use of AI.

Specificity is a valuable heuristic here, too, pulled from JMM email theory. I've seen SaaS proposals focused on a single use case work wonders. They thrive within hyper-minimal "commercials" on the pricing page literally set to "tranche-based" or just a single, precise figure of 634K.

In enterprise sales, often nailing a single use-case is far more important than taking on all the issues your various clients might want to achieve. Such was the case with instant surveys for an airline app.

Chapter 3: Closing - Perception meets Reality

"CLOSING" is a loaded topic. Clients aren't acquired; they're created. Always and only through conversation.

I used to believe that if you didn't close a deal, it was simply an indication of messing up the sales process somewhere earlier. Then I traveled with Garrett "The G.O.A.T." MacDonald selling mobile technology, and learned that "closing skills" are very real, albeit an anomaly. GMAC could basically get blood from a stone. On several occasions I witnessed him turn a "cigar with one puff left" (Buffett) into a home run!

A winning strategy begins early by being paranoid. Identify:

    a.   A compelling event
    b.   The correct consensus
    c.   Shared value - stakeholder alignment on why to buy
    d.   A compelling ROI-focused business case / quantifying the upside. Do they know when they'll break even / exceed 3X return (often an F500 procurement requirement)
    e.   Budget allocation or ability to pull budget from another P&L
    f.   A strong compelling reason/event: yep, I listed it twice! If they don't do this now, will the wheels come off, the house burn down, and who will get fired?

This is why deals frequently close for me - because I cover all these vectors plus POLITICAL factors.

I hate to break it to you, but B2B negotiation is actually *nothing like* a hostage crisis. We often don't even have an active hostage despite thinking we have a captive audience, however ornery. ;-)

I invented "de-threading" because many deals wither away on the main email chain. The decay rate or Steve Chandler's "half-life of enthusiasm" is a big deal. You must progress sales post-demo (or 'a verbal') assertively to create urgency, or they will die on the vine. I take each stakeholder off the primary "check-in" email thread to *de-thread*. "Hey, how was the meeting/demo for you?" Perhaps they're dealing with a new competitor pulled from a last-minute Google search.

My favorite *Maverick Method* Brian Burns quote remains, "What is not covertly positive is overtly negative." Nature abhors a vacuum. When your opportunities go dark, nothing good can come from it. Nobody ever has a great date, then waits three months to tell you.

Avoid "over-closing the close."

An early mentor of mine was big on this idea. Legend has it that sales trainers in the '50s, even back to the '20s, used to yell at audiences, "Shut up!" to prevent this destructive practice.

Stop selling once you get the polarity shift and the desire is built in the prospect's world. Once you start getting buying signals, get off the call as fast as you can. Remember, questions - even objections - can be a strong buying signal. Give CXOs the greatest gift: time. Ten minutes back on their calendar. Keep them wanting more.

If you have five slides and they are chomping at the bit on slide three, end the meeting and ask if they'd like another set of stakeholders to see the demo. If you really want to get a rise out of a serious group, like I shared earlier, bring 60ish slides and once they grimace, relieve them with, "Don't worry, I'll just hit the top 5."

We must catch and release in this deep-sea fishing scenario. If your marlin gets hooked, let out the line. Reel too fast in any deal stage; you'll snap it, turning off your prospect, possibly for good. I see this so frequently in the application of RRM (route-ruin-multiply), my signature call opener which is non-PBO (permission-based). The prospect mentions a pain, and the seller just spoon-feeds their solution with sugar, Mary Poppins style.

Don't ever put an immediate band-aid on the wound. Poke the wound, and twist the knife. (Scott Britton) SPIN questions are still the key, even if you identify minor irritation. Where there's smoke, there's fire.

Why aren't your deals closing? No pain = no urgency, no meeting, no sale. Be a painkiller, not a vitamin.

You need to probe enough and go into full-blown Columbo mode. I love how Jeff Thull encourages you to become a doctor, detective, and therapist. Most discovery calls these days are too sunny; they're skin deep.

"You need to dive 10,000 leagues under the ocean and know what they ate for breakfast last Tuesday." – Jim Mongillo

Another major reason your deals don't close is that you aren't "asking for the business." To quote former football player turned Salesforce legend Tom Radle, "Look them in the eyes and state confidently, 'I am going to transform your business.'"

"Presentation without discovery is sales malpractice." – Mike Weinberg

When we sell the dream, we must find the goal *behind* the goal. The prospect is on a default path which could be a downward or upward spiral. Werner Erhard's revelation posits a model where you "create your future from your future, not your past." Mantra: You are not your story: the false narrative you tell about yourself. You are your potential. The future is always unlimited.

We need to understand intimately what's driving our prospects and their deeper motivations. We need to air out the baggage from when they tried to solve this problem internally (or with other vendors). To quote Steve Chandler, "Leave every conversation in a context of possibility, not price."

I'll never forget doing a 600K 2-year deal on the last day of Q4, working up until midnight with our General Counsel and E-Team on New Year's Eve. We were thrilled to displace 5 of our competitors with a TCO reduction sale. Our platform consolidated many competing offerings, and point solutions, lowering 'total cost of ownership.'

There were literally 243 interactions, including jokingly threatening to call Jeffrey Katzenberg to steal his team. The CXO was a former Coast Guard lieutenant. We attempted many 3-way cold calls, some of which backfired, but we pressed on with humor and alacrity undeterred into the night.

When we finally closed the deal on a small concession so "he could school his people on old-school negotiation," all he could admit was, "I read every email you wrote thinking, 'You guys are either insane or I have to work with you.'" I highlight another axiom in the JMM:

Interactivity is the only currency of effective outbound. Hence, a negative response is still positive.

To share another classic closing moment, I remember getting lunch in San Francisco with a prospect - very satisfied with their strategy of having a half-dozen mobile marketing vendors spliced together into a Frankenstack. He was even bragging about what a massive budget his CEO gave him to buy shiny new toys because he crushed top line revenue growth by 30X since hired a few years ago.

We challenged him with the idea that it didn't matter how many vendors he collected if he lost 40% of his monthly active users (MAU) to fraud, and explained our algorithms could eliminate that problem.

In brutal dead-stop traffic, we ended up in an A/C-less Uber for 90 minutes (each way!) from SF to Menlo Park. We wandered into the conference room, exhausted and with sweaty collars, where the prospect's marketing team had assembled begrudgingly.

We looked them directly in their eyes and verbally proposed like a base jump, "1.XMM dollars." You could hear a pin drop. Our main stakeholder warned, "If you say that number one more time, I'll kick you out of the building. That's more than our entire tech stack per year!" This was an intense "extreme high-anchor" moment, but we still did North of a half-million-dollar deal with a sick margin off the back of it.

Let clients experience the value of your coaching/consulting/solution before they buy.

This analogy is also looked at similarly to the "Island Parable" by Carolyn Freyer-Jones. Your prospect is on one island and they want to reach another, better one with fresh water and low coconuts. ;-) You must be that boat or bridge to help them reach their target faster.

New mantra: "We will sail together. I will help you navigate."

Here's a unique 7-Step Process to close a consulting services engagement, coaching call, or software deal. It leverages the distinction of "default future vs. created future" as I mentioned before:

1. Find out exactly what they want to achieve: "What is your goal?" (usually monetary, like 500K income, or 3-5X pipeline, or getting promoted to VP in under 6 months)
2. Find out what's driving that "want" (the goal behind the goal - hint: it's seldom only money) - e.g., get out of debt. Ask questions to clarify-refine: *Why don't you think you've hit it? What do you think is limiting you?) (h/t Scott Leese Addiction Model - they must first admit to pain in order to create a clearing for change. Note: people hate/ fear change.)*
3. Ask, "What else have you tried?" to clear out the baggage of "the ex-significant other" problem. Always positively acknowledge it. *Once you've done a controlled burn, a new forest can grow. You've instilled them with HOPE again and hope is one of the most powerful forces in the universe right behind love, curiosity, and admiration: all elements of this system!*
4. Ask, "What's been holding you back?" Listen deeply... Then explain your failures - your vulnerability story painting the before-and-after picture. Tell them how this solution worked for you.
5. Explain precisely how you can help them hit their goal based on how you have helped others (social proof) but always CUSTOMIZE the story to them.

6. Let them ask for the pricing. (Indicates desire aka polarity shift.)
7. Always leave them in the context of dreams and possibility - aka investing in achieving their desired goals and outcomes in Step 1. Don't leave them stressing about affordability (price).

If you're still hazy, ask, "What would make this exactly the (coaching/consulting/solution) you're looking for?" Whatever they mention, answer, "Perhaps I can assist you with that."

To prevent decay rate, follow up shortly after with references and testimonials, preferably with a video or screenshot. Encourage them to contact your references. Nobody does that!

It's a Blountism: People buy you. Your customers close your deals. You don't.

Clients invest in your ability to either help them reach the goal, increase their chances of success, or speed up their velocity.

Once I truly feel I've closed, I drop my favorite Hormozi, "Why wouldn't you move forward?" Pressure test any "yes!"

All the gold is in the word CUSTOMIZE.

CUSTOMIZED GUIDANCE is the key to closing consulting. Ensure your strategy is CUSTOMIZED to their challenges, tailored to their business case. Phrases like "hold you accountable" highlight the value of investing in an expert.

NOBODY buys coaching; they buy the result of coaching. They don't buy the hammer, nail, or picture hanger. They want a beautiful painting on the wall. Your reasons don't matter, only theirs. Therefore, focus on your prospect's dream outcome and what's driving it.

"My fees are a commitment to weed out the uncommitted." - Steve Chandler

What's your guarantee? Well, I'd never make a hard performance guarantee for coaching; that's fraud. YOU must lift the weights in the gym yourself; the trainer can't do it for you like a marionette. See the point? Ultimately people are paying for my time, but I have clients that go bold on that with Hormozi/Brunson/Kennedy verbiage – so explore it. Ask if you can honestly defend it. Enterprise folks reading this will often be forced to include service-level agreements (SLAs) - check with your CTO to ensure they are standard vs. egregious; often five-nines (99.999%) uptime can sync you especially when it includes penalties by the hour.

Selling services is a unique beast. My 1:1 coaching isn't a course or offer; it's strategic consulting. "You bring the will. I can improve your skill." Remember to share with everyone you meet, that coaching worked for you. A coach without a coach is like a brain surgeon who won't see a surgeon to remove a tumor. That's why I started this book with "sales is the transference" of belief. If you aren't passionate about the product, and convinced that it "solved the problem" for you, why would anyone buy what you're selling?

That's why salespeople that used to be a client of the thing they sell, crush it.

Now let's tune into a product pitch or demo stage. We notice that this law of selling needs to be addressed for beauty pageants, dog & pony shows, name drops, popularity contests, and feature-dumping manager "super-closes." We've lost touch with what drives sales and basic human behavior. Our prospects want to fix their problems and achieve immediate outcomes (ROI). They need our help.

Don't try to hard-close on the first call. Realize: everything in a recession is now relegated to a "considered purchase." Lately, I've been shocked to see a president's signature on a nominal routine contract.

Be empathetic and mindful of your prospect's situation. Encourage them to check with their partner. Sleep on it.

Don't just be willing to walk: walk.

CORNER CASES & TROUBLESHOOTING:

Can you believe that sometimes deals don't close because the prospect is intimidated by the consultant? The prospect thinks: "Am I good enough to be coached?" "Do I have the time or capacity to do this?" or even: "JM can do this, but I can't."

Those are some of the fears you need to address to get the sale. Your prospects own hidden negative self-talk. Uncover the fears your prospects are scared to share, and put them at ease.

4th frame selling is like unlocking and walking through a series of gates. Most people get hung up on step #4 and #5.

1. Initiate chat
2. Pull to zoom
3. Go deep
4. Emotionally connect
5. Polarity shifts
6. Share fee positioned to the ROI of achieving their dream

Scotty Hennessy edition:

1. Gauge where they're at
2. Desired outcome?

3. Challenges getting there?
4. Why it's important
5. What happens if the situation stays the same?
6. 2-minute pitch
7. Handle objections
8. Close

#5 creates urgency and scarcity - reminiscent of Brent Adamson's, "pain of the same is greater than the pain of change." This is hugely important. No fear = no change.

Part of helping your clients overcome their fears is learning how to address your own concerns. For many coaches, this starts by banishing imposter syndrome, and taking ownership of your value.

Practice saying your fee out loud and in the mirror. Whenever you convey your rate to a prospect, immediately validate it, by tying it to their anticipated ROI and their goals. Validate your value, and respect it.

I once coached a client that did almost everything in this book exactly right. In his first coaching/consulting calls, he shared all of his knowledge expertly, gave massive amounts of value, and engaged his prospects.

But the deals weren't closing.

Why?

Because the "value of coaching" is mainly, "being heard," and being "understood." Transformation is in the eye of the beholder - the experience your client has *being* with you. Sometimes that differentiator is simply: "presence." That's why the "health of the healer" is so important in coaching.

Work on you: be the change you wish to see in the world. Testimonials are imperative to effective closing. Your prospects believe in you based on the results you help others achieve, not what you claim to offer with your marketing campaigns. They're certainly not swayed by diplomas on your wall.

Remember, giving too much value straight away can be dangerous. Sometimes it's too early to give away the plot line in the trailer in the first 10 minutes when you meet. There's a special place in hell for people who read books from the ending first.

Patience always solves.

Earn their trust, meet most situations with powerful silence, keep asking "why?" This ensures your prospects will feel "heard," maybe for the first time in their lives. They'll open up. They'll trust you. They'll want to pay you for more. Most of my intake calls are 25 minutes of client talking, and 5 minutes of the best possible questions I can craft from the gut and heart... in the moment.

Be fully there.

If you waste too much time spewing technobabble and tactics, you'll overwhelm your client and they'll feel they couldn't possibly do the whole program, or that they don't need more consulting. Look how much more homework is on their plate.

You need to unburden them, not add more weight. Successful selling is always about *reducing friction*.

A first call is discovery not delivery. It's a diagnostic process, just like a doctor evaluating the symptoms of a patient. Do a full intake and take inventory where you find out every last issue and problem your prospect has, and explore ways you could help them. Then boldly ask for your fee and if they don't pay it, catch and release.

Conveying the value of your solution: coaching, consulting, service, software platform or trusted advice does *not* mean divulging all your secrets before they've paid you. It means actively listening, caring and planning how you could indeed solve issues for your prospect synergistically (1 + 1 = 11) were they to hire you.

Growing your practice, a spiritual path of service:

Did you know that the brain has something called neuroplasticity, or the ability to evolve, even into your 90s? No matter how traumatic, your childhood does not permanently define your personality. Per James Clear, you can drop almost any habit within 66 days – most people don't know it and stay a prisoner of their story, never realizing how malleable their neurons can be.

The secret to effective enrollment (client acquisition) is to share your growth and evolution doing this. Discuss and explore the concept of impermanence and how it relates to the potential for change.

Your past experiences do not define you. You are not the initial chapters of your story. You write your narrative and determine who you'll become.

You can develop new habits – new grooves in your brain's neuroplasticity (synaptic patterns firing) – and make changes for a better future from your future, despite what others may lead you to believe. That's why coaching works.

We must shift from being self-conscious to having a service mindset.

The amount you charge for your services depends on the size and urgency of the problem you are solving. It's reasonable to charge a higher fee to solve a million-dollar problem. It's all about finding balance. You need to ensure you don't overcharge your clients and make them feel exploited. On the other hand, charging too little may leave you resentful, with even more problems.

Remember to appreciate your work's impact and not take yourself too seriously. Ultimately, you are a valuable instrument in helping others, guided by a higher power.

The value you deliver is in giving people the ability to achieve transformation and change.

If your fear of charging your clients the right price is holding you back, you'll never make any real progress.

To change your relationship with money, it's essential to let go of any emotional attachment to it, including feelings of anger and fear. Remember that money is simply a number and a means of accessing the fruits of your labor.

It's important to depersonalize your relationship with money and let go of old beliefs or fears, such as the idea that money is the 'root of all evil.' By doing so, you can develop a more rational, reality-based understanding of your finances.

Changing your relationship with money also changes how you think about your profession. If you want to feel fulfilled in this world, you need to fall in love with what you do - guiding others.

How can you possibly succeed at prospecting and building pipeline effectively when you hate it? The beauty is hate is the polar opposite of love and many of my clients now adore the process, and are even addicted to it, because they can approach it in a new way. Convert your hate into rocket fuel that allows you to fall in love with creating clients.

Impossible, you say? My theory of everything is: hold as many meaningful conversations with your dream clients as you can and you'll never suffer or work another day of your life in new business sales. That my friends, is prospecting Nirvana (and completely possible within your new paradigm of 4th frame and RRM modalities).

I love what I do, and I promise you I'm not a space alien (or pathological liar), contrary to the popular belief of a few scattered haters. Yes, I burnt out sometimes after grinding outbound for the first 15 years, but for the last 7, since I embraced curiosity/love-based approaches – still prospecting every day – everything became zen.

Avoid any natural aversion to transacting and overcome any fear of money by embracing your entire business holistically - even the pricing side.

Never discuss price in an email. "What are your fees?" they ask. Deflect and realign: "We have packages for every budget, why don't we hop on a call to discuss your goals?" Always handle the money conversation face-to-face (or voice-to-voice).

When scheduling conversations, keep it simple, and don't let your ego, survival instincts, or self-esteem get in the way.

Focus on mutually enjoyable dialogue between both parties and mark it on your calendar in two colors. My day is simple. Give and serve. "Blue = serving clients. Purple = creating clients (still by serving)." Hat tip to Rich Litvin.

Modifying our belief systems is necessary, as negative and inaccurate perceptions don't align with reality. A good practice is to affirm your worth and value, even out-loud daily. Accepting cash for services rendered can be challenging, but it's how life works.

Coming at customers with a negative mindset may hinder your ability to close the deal. On the other hand, bringing a positive attitude and a clear view of your value cuts like a hot knife.

It's paramount to forgive yourself and others to avoid holding onto grudges and resentments. Research has shown that anger can negatively impact your health and ability to manifest your goals. Make a list and bury the hatchet, even if you can't reach them.

Make meeting with prospects a game and you'll close far more. Enjoy the thrill ride it can be! Here's a wild new game from Melissa Ford: "Imagine you can never close this person, only serve them." How would you spend the first hour if you eliminated the profit motive? New avenues of giving and service emerge and paradoxically, prospects sense this, causing the polarity to shift even faster.

Chapter 4: Find Your AI Superpower

"AI ever allows us to truly understand ourselves, it will not be because these algorithms capture the mechanical essence of the human mind. It will be because they liberated us to forget about optimizations and to instead focus on what truly makes us human: loving and being loved." – Kai-Fu Lee

Greg Meyer is a leading expert in product management for Open AI & GPT engineering. He's what niche enthusiasts call an "AI Whisperer."

Naturally, I had to get him on board for the AI experiments in this book. Formerly my colleague and Data Czar at OutboundWorks (acquired), he has held high-level Product & RevOps positions at Redis & Syncari.

He is now running Data & Ops, a fractional product practice. He's this book's technical editor, focused on ensuring the advice contained herein is future-proof. In the coming decades, the JMM must stand up to the breakneck speed of artificial intelligence innovation, wave after wave, without triggering your internal "B.S. alarm" too much.

Here's how *we* future-proof ourselves from the AI-assisted outbound craze: by differentiating our GPT prompts from everyone else's by incorporating our individual uniqueness and tone. In a few words, it's essential to amplify the things that make you (the human being) unique.

What you will be doing with this method is using GPT as an extension of your own thinking, rather than expecting the computer to do all the work (and getting half-baked results). You will be asking it for input, and then—as the human being that you are–modifying that input to further refine its output and get ever closer to exactly what you want.

If you're new to chatbots, here are a few prompts to try as a seller:

1. "Craft a catchy cold email template to grab potential clients' attention and get them interested in our B2B product or service."
2. "Share tips for quickly sizing up and prioritizing B2B leads to focus on the most promising prospects."
3. "List common B2B buyer hesitations and advise on how to tackle them like a pro."
4. "Give pointers on building lasting B2B client relationships through great communication and ongoing value."
5. "Offer a game plan for nailing a B2B product demo that connects with the audience and showcases our solution's benefits."

Something to remember when you're composing your prompts: AI is matching probabilities, not thinking. When it completes the next word, it is finding the most likely outcome based on the context of the information you shared.

This means you need to add context. Use short, declarative sentences and sequential steps to help the AI provide answers closer to your needs. Don't be afraid to ask it to edit or revise. "Make this simpler to read," "Rephrase this in the inspirational style of Nike advertising," or "Condense this to 100 words," are all examples of prompts that will improve your result.

Here's a quick superpower you can build with AI: Ask it to play a game where you sequentially add information and stop to refine it if you have questions.

Use this initial prompt:

> Let's play a game where I ask you to suggest some prompts I could ask ChatGPT to help me think through some business problems.
>
> You will know we are playing the game when I start the conversation with [robot emoji, star emoji] and follow that with the topic I want to discuss.
>
> You respond with this answer "[robot emoji, star emoji] I'm ready to play the game! Please provide the topic you want to discuss, and we can generate prompts to help you think through your business problems."
>
> An example prompt is this: "Please describe the specific problem you are currently working on as a B2B SaaS account executive or sales manager and identify the key metric you are focusing on to solve this issue."
>
> Here is an example context to add to the prompt: "This information will help us provide relevant operational questions and best practices tailored to your situation, including growth strategies and insights from SaaS sales veterans like Mark Roberge, writer of *The Sales Acceleration Formula*."

When you are ready to explore in more depth, remember as you compose, say "enhance the answer" followed by the question number.

I will respond with the emoji [robot emoji, checked box emoji] to confirm that we are providing more detail for the selected question and then help you iteratively answer it.

If I need you to change the context, I will respond [robot emoji, high voltage emoji] and you will ask me for information about the context.

To end the game, I will write: [robot emoji, microphone emoji, down arrow emoji] and you will return to normal functioning.

To confirm you understand these instructions, respond: "[hundred points emoji]Let's Play[hundred points emoji]"

After you enter these words, ChatGPT will respond:

[hundred points emoji]Let's Play[hundred points emoji]

You can then write a relevant question, like:

[robot emoji, star emoji] Please help me with some prompts to improve the readability of my cold emails

(Note: using the emoji token helps the bot know we are playing the game)

Here's one of the superpowers added by this prompt: you can tell the bot to "Enhance the answer for item 3" or any other ordered or unordered item in the list of answers.

Now, you've created a super coach – think of this as your "Jarvis," Tony Stark's badass AI assistant – that you can use to help you solve problems.

There are a few guardrails to consider:

1. Don't share private information using the OpenAI API
2. Do expect this information to be indexed by the bot
3. Have fun!

Here's another prompt you can try to assist you in prospecting. This one iteratively prompts you to refine your "personal ask" as you approach senior leaders during a prospecting loop.

Let's play a game: pretend you are an early-stage VC-backed SaaS CEO or senior leader in GTM at a leading SaaS company.

I will start the game by writing [insert emojis]

Examples include companies with the kind of initial growth rates like Airtable, Notion, and Loom; they are typically 50-500 employees in size and have 5-20MM in annual revenue, multi-provider business model is SaaS, and they employ product-led growth (PLG) tactics to help trial customers graduate into paying customers.

Please ask me 3-4 questions to help me identify a bullet-pointed personal skills inventory. Then, prompt me to identify the industry, company size, and a few sample companies where I might like to work.

Then please prompt me with 2-3 examples of companies and ask me whether they fall into that preferred set of companies.

After each prompt, pause and ask me to answer or skip that question, then continue.

You will know when to continue when I end my answer with [insert emojis]

Once I select a company, give me a table containing the following columns: name, summary, key challenges, competitors where:

- name includes the company name

- a summary is a 50-word summary of the company

- key challenges is a 50-word summary of the company's key challenges

- competitors: list their top 3 competitors in bullet form

After that, suggest a 50-100 word targeted ask I could make to that company's leader to ask for potential employment.

Ask me to revise this prompt with my own words or updated instructions, then modify it.

You will know when to continue when I end my answer with [insert emojis]

Example prompt 1:

"I looked at your first-time user experience for product X. There are several ways to improve it. Examples include a, b, and c. Open to a conversation?"

Example prompt 2:

"Do you know someone who needs <the targeted service we identified earlier in the prompt>")

Please respond with " [insert emojis]Let's Go [insert emojis]" to confirm you understand these instructions.

When I write [insert emojis], the game is over, and we can return to standard processing.

One of the most important pieces of advice I can give you is this. Stop running from AI and learn to love the bots.

"AI is going to take our jobs" is a constant refrain.

But maybe it's more accurate to say that AI *will take the most tedious parts of our jobs*. Plus, let's face it, it's not like anyone can avoid AI forever. If you don't learn how to use the latest tech yourself, someone else will. Adapt or die, as they say.

GPT is a transformational technology.

It *will* change the way we live and work - it's inevitable.

Working *with* the bots, not against them, will require a new way of thinking. But it's not all that different from adapting to the latest technology we've encountered over the last few years.

Here are a few ways software building and personal development are changing because of GPT-style tools:

1. We need a private tutor to teach us how to talk to computers. *Asking an AI to complete a procedure (currently) differs from talking to someone.*
2. This is a fundamental shift from "company-designed software" to "personal-designed software." *The software that makes you a 10X seller will look radically different from the software that works for others.*
3. We are going to need to get better at security. *If you need to share private information with a tool like this, you'll*

need a private vector database to store your embeddings (the data used to build a large language model or LLM).

4. We will need to be able to authenticate as a human or a robot. *Distinguishing between people and machines will become harder.*

5. We are going to need our own AI personal assistants. *Imagine what it would be like to ask a virtual assistant to do your work, knowing that it can follow instructions accurately and ask for feedback.*

We need software to help teach us how to build software. It's tough to get your head around, I know. But as humans, we've encountered similar revolutionary paths before.

For a simple analogy, consider the switch from "dumb" mobile phones to the iPhone. At first, this new thing seemed like a toy, and then it was pretty neat, and then it became an indispensable part of the working toolkit for just about everyone.

This network effect will also happen with GPT. It's difficult to see where the winds of change will take us right now. GPT is going to be transformational- we just don't know exactly how the world will evolve yet.

What begins today as a toolkit for building marketable copy could soon become a hand-held digital Sun Tzu of business strategy.

What's an intelligent technologist to do?

Simple: learn how to use your tools.

For AI, that will mean building AI for *you* and not using a generic prompt that works the same for every user. Optimize the prompts to use your strengths, and you will create a tool that helps augment your own skills and lessens your weaknesses.

Here's a step-by-step framework to train AI to recognize *your* prompts:

1. Get comfortable with whatever process you document. Imagine that you will be a conductor or orchestrator for that action. The prompt needs to give the model enough information to ingest and respond to. This means it might involve multiple steps.
2. Then, investigate the AI or model you are informing and learn how to adjust your syntax accordingly. For a tool like ChatGPT, this means using a declarative sentence or paragraph to give it context:
   o *"Given the company at Microsoft.com, summarize the business strategy and identify the departments most likely to handle a channel inquiry to become a technology partner. Find the VP or Director of that department. If you encounter multiple answers, create them as a table with the following columns: Department name, website, description, key contacts, name, email, phone number"*
3. You might not get the answer you need, so prompt it with a follow-up, e.g., "Imagine that you are an SDR and need to look up this information and populate the table"
4. Note that the first response you receive might not be entirely accurate. AI solutions aren't always trained on real-time data. However, a strategy like this can build a summary table or a place for others to fill in or validate data in a fraction of the time required for research.
5. Don't use copy-paste. The purpose of these tools is *not* to replace your brain - it's to do the initial "busy work" so you can focus on the creative work.

If you only get vague or limited results, ask ChatGPT to expand on specific sections. Provide more detail about what you want, and keep pushing until you get a more comprehensive document.

Here are a few more insights to keep in mind from David Young-blood:

1. **Embrace Personalization:** Discover how to personalize AI-generated content to establish stronger connections with your target audience. Add your own flair to whatever ChatGPT spits back vs. leveraging it verbatim.
2. **Master Predictive Analytics:** Uncover the power of predictive analytics in forecasting sales trends, customer behavior, and market dynamics. Turn ChatGPT and similar tools into your personal research team.
3. **Amplify Customer Experience:** Delve into the realm of AI-powered customer experience enhancement. Learn how to leverage chatbots and virtual assistants to keep the conversation going and inspire customer loyalty.
4. **Data-Driven Sales Strategies:** Harness the potential of big data and AI to develop data-driven sales strategies. Feed your generative AI tool all the data it needs to provide you with useful strategies and insights.
5. **Ethical Considerations:** Navigate the ethical implications of AI in sales and business. Understand the importance of transparency, fairness, and accountability when leveraging AI technologies.
6. **Reinventing Sales Enablement:** Revolutionize your sales enablement strategies with AI. Learn how to leverage intelligent sales tools, automate processes, and empower your sales team to drive results.

7. **Embracing AI in Lead Generation:** Discover how AI can revolutionize lead generation by identifying high-potential prospects, automating lead qualification, and streamlining the sales pipeline.

8. **AI-Powered Sales Forecasting:** Dive into the world of AI-powered sales forecasting. Understand how advanced algorithms can analyze historical data, market trends, and external factors to generate accurate sales predictions.

In summary, use AI to reinforce what makes you a unique seller (and human being). Use it as a fantastic research agent. But don't use it to replace your efforts. If you want to dive deeper into the subject, you can also check out Greg Meyer's website. (DatanOps. com)

GPT Lab: practicing MEDDIC

Practice your MEDDIC (Metrics, Economic Buyer, Decision Criteria, Decision Process, Identify Pain, and Champion) process by Dick Dunkel.

You can send three prompts to a GPT process to help you refine your MEDDIC strategy:

1. "You are a world-class seller who knows the MEDDIC framework. What's the best way to find the main decision-maker and get their needs and pain points?"
2. "How can I quickly determine what matters most to my prospect and make my solution stand out?"
3. "Any tips for teaming up with insiders at a prospect's company to help close the deal?"

Unleashing the Power of AI

Contributed by Soham Sarkar, Co-Founder and Head of Prompt Design, Namora.ai

This section comes to you from an incredible AI guru, who I worked with on the creation of this book, specifically to help you unlock the potential of advanced AI messaging for B2B. After all, artificial intelligence is bound to become a crucial part of the sales cycle going forward.

According to Soham, Large Language Models (LLMs) like GPT-4 have revolutionized natural language processing, bringing transformative applications to various fields, including sales.

Use cases range from automating lead generation and enhancing customer support to streamlining email drafting and creating intelligent chatbots.

Here's your guide to the inner workings of LLMs, their specific applications in sales, and the best practices for harnessing their power effectively.

THE MECHANICS OF LLMS

LLMs, such as GPT-4, process and understand vast amounts of text data to generate coherent and fluent responses. They employ deep learning techniques based on the Transformer architecture, which empowers them to process text data in parallel, making it more computationally efficient than older designs like recurrent neural networks (RNNs).

Through self-attention and positional encoding mechanisms, LLMs are not only capable of capturing long-range relationships within the text but also accounting for the order of these relationships. This makes the Transformer architecture the backbone of modern LLMs that work with text inputs like emails, chat logs, articles, and generate relevant outputs.

MASTERING THE ART OF PROMPTING

Prompting is the primary interface between users and Large Language Models. It involves crafting a question, statement, or input that guides the AI model to generate the desired output. Effective use of prompting techniques ensures the system's response aligns with the users' expectations and context.

To extract maximum value from LLMs, sales representatives can leverage various prompting techniques. Each technique serves a unique purpose and helps address different challenges that sales reps face daily:

1. ZERO-SHOT PROMPTING:

The LLM uses its foundational knowledge to tackle questions or tasks it wasn't trained on explicitly. For example, a sales rep using GPT-4 to craft an email targeting an industry-specific audience without supplying prior examples related to that industry.

When writing a 'zero shot' prompt it's important not to overload the model with too much context. Keep your instructions and tasks within a limited scope and as small as possible.

Remember you are essentially telling the model "Do X" and you have no way of verifying how well it will do that job.

2. CHAIN OF THOUGHT PROMPTING:

This technique involves constructing a sequence of connected thoughts or actions to arrive at a solution. A sales rep might ask GPT-4 to create a step-by-step plan to increase lead conversions.

Tip - Use the phrase "let's think step by step" or provide 2-3 examples of breaking down the solution in sub-steps.

At a technical level, CoT works exceptionally well because of how language models work.

Here is a helpful abstraction - Every new token (roughly a word) generated is the model "thinking".

The beauty of 'chain of thought' prompting is that the model ends up 'thinking' to a degree while it's generating the answer. It's dynamically thinking!

So how do you maximize this?

When you are writing the prompt instruction to the model you must give it a framework to reason i.e "think about problem X like…"

More on this in the next technique!

3. STEP-BY-STEP PROMPTING:

With this strategy, a problem is decomposed into smaller steps, with LLMs progressively solving these steps. This method is ideal for troubleshooting customer issues by guiding them through a process one step at a time.

Step-by-step prompting is similar to 'Chain of Thought' but much more powerful. While chain of thought prompting involves giving the model a reasoning framework and telling it to "think step-by-step", SbS prompt quite literally gives the model the "steps."

Imagine you are researching an account - you have general account data such as firmographics, financials, and some relevant news and linkedin data.

In a SbS prompt you would include 2-5 examples or training companies before giving the model the actual company you want the generation for.

For each of the examples you would guide the model to the solution in the given format:

Step 1: <Reason>
Step 2: <Reason>...
Step N: <Therefore, Solution>

Here the Steps 1 to N are teaching the model how to "think" about this particular problem type. It's a bit heavy on the prompt consumption but extremely worth it.

4. REASONING STAGES PROMPTING:

Through this technique, LLMs gradually build a solution that incorporates information from prior steps. This approach can be applied to help sales reps analyze customer responses to identify potential objections and build persuasive arguments.

Tip - Create a stage-based reasoning system similar to CoT or Step-by-Step but each stage can have multiple sub steps

Stage-based reasoning is a more dynamic version of Step-by-Step and one that retains most of the benefits without using as many tokens.

The biggest difference is you replace "Steps" for "Stages".

So what's the difference between "Steps" and "Stages"?

While "Steps" were explicit instructions to the language model to tell it 'how' to think, "Stages" are protocols to 'make' them think. You are leveraging the billions of neural networks the model already possesses for them to run millions of scenarios about your problem in a second and letting it think of the best responses.

Let's revisit the previous example of conducting account research. In this situation instead of creating reasoning steps by providing examples, we will create reasoning stages that will act like logical thought processes.

Here is the cool part, subsequent stages are activated based on the reasoning of the previous stages and can act like filters.

Let's start with a simple 3-stage reasoning protocol for the same account research problem statement by adding the given stages in the prompt.

Stage 1: Does the given account have any relevant information that would indicate them being a good fit for my company?
Stage 2: Is it relevant to how I sell my product?
Stage 3: Are there any better alternatives?

When the model returns the response you will find that it will not only answer your question but give you its reasoning for coming to its answer.

By the time it gets to the last stage it will even reformulate its answer based on Stage 1 and 2.

Example - if it used a non-relevant sales trigger for Stage 1 and it would review the information in Stage 2 and conclude it's not a great trigger to use and think of alternatives. By Stage 3 you would get a much better response.

5. SELF-REFLECTION PROMPTING:

This method trains the LLM to evaluate its responses, identifying errors or room for improvement, thereby enhancing its understanding of the problem. A sales rep may use GPT-4 to refine an initial draft of an email campaign, for instance.

Tip - Ask the LLM to provide feedback on the output as the final output. Combine this with Reasoning Stages with the "final stage" being the self critique steps.

6. PERSONA ADOPTION PROMPTING:

With this method distinct character or communication style is created for the LLM, generating responses that align with that persona. This technique is useful for tailoring content, like email campaigns, to a sales rep's specific brand voice or target audience.

7. ROLEPLAY PROMPTING:

This model follows a scenario or roleplay to generate contextually relevant outputs. In a sales environment, a chatbot could be developed, simulating a sales rep's conversation with a potential customer for training purposes.

8. DIALOGUE OPTIMIZATION PROMPTING:

This approach focuses on improving the quality of generated chatbot dialogues or conversations. For example, a company could create a customer support chatbot that intelligently responds to varied customer issues.

9. Labeling Prompting:

By adding metadata like tags or categories to prompts, the LLM gains additional context. In a sales landscape, these labels could include product categories or customer personas.

10. K-Shot Prompting:

The model is provided with K examples of the desired outcome, refining its understanding of the task and its ability to produce accurate responses. For instance, K examples of well-drafted sales outreach emails can help guide GPT-4 to create a new batch of personalized and effective sales emails.

11. Context Stuffing Prompting:

This technique adds extra context to a prompt, influencing the power of the AI-generated response. A sales rep may use past conversations with a customer to develop personalized follow-up emails, for instance.

Maximizing the Impact of LLMs in Sales

LLMs can assist sales representatives with a wide array of tasks, such as drafting emails, generating leads, providing customer support, managing chatbots, and more. However, be prepared for occasional irrelevant or inaccurate responses. LLMs aren't perfect yet, and they require a great deal of training to perform effectively. It's also worth being mindful of the ethical implications related to biases and misinformation.

BEST PRACTICES FOR HARNESSING THE POWER OF LLMs

While working with LLMs, it's crucial to:

1. **Provide clear and specific instructions to guide the LLM:** Be straightforward and direct. For instance, you might create a concise request for GPT-4 to create a list of product benefits tailored to a particular customer persona. *"Please create a list of product benefits related to this persona."*

2. **Supply the LLM with relevant examples and ample context:** The more context you can provide, the easier it is to ensure the desired outputs align closely with your specific requirements.

3. **Experiment with different types of prompting techniques based on the context, outcome, and unique factors in each situation:** Experimentation is an excellent way to improve the outcomes you get from your large language models. Just like you'd experiment with different pitching techniques in sales, don't be afraid to get creative when using generative AI.

4. **Regularly monitor and assess the AI-generated content to ensure accuracy, relevance, and consistency:** It might even be worth taking notes outlining which prompt styles and strategies work best for your needs.

UNDERSTANDING AND MITIGATING HALLUCINATIONS

Hallucinations can be a common concern in the generative AI landscape. When bots are dealing with huge amounts of data, it's easy for things to go awry, particularly if you're not careful.

Hallucinations occur when LLMs generate content that is irrelevant or inaccurate. They often result from uncertainty about the provided prompt or the task's context. To reduce hallucinations, provide clear instructions and additional context to guide the LLM.

OVERCOMING MEMORY LIMITATIONS

The lack of long-term memory capabilities in LLMs proves challenging for maintaining coherence in the generated content.

Techniques like context stuffing and reinforcement learning with human feedback [RLHF]—where the LLM adjusts its output based on the input of a human evaluator—help improve LLMs' memory capabilities.

OPTIMIZING TOKEN UTILIZATION

LLMs consume tokens (words/sub-words) during text generation. Efficient token consumption ensures better performance and accuracy.

Optimal token utilization can be achieved by applying effective prompt engineering techniques, such as instruction supply, to LLMs.

THE FUTURE OF LLMS IN SALES

The future of LLMs in sales is promising. Some companies are now focusing on developing LLM agents that can revolutionize sales processes and improve efficiency across the board.

These LLM agents have the potential to become invaluable tools for sales reps as they adapt to new challenges and leverage AI-driven insights.

While they might not be able to replace the human sales representative entirely, they can act as a useful assistant.

In the SaaS industry specifically, sales professionals can leverage LLMs to improve their cold email outreach, account and persona research, and messaging strategies.

For example, autonomous AI agents powered by LLMs can conduct research on behalf of SDRs, identifying prospects, gathering industry insights, and tailoring content to a specific target audience.

These agents can also assist in copywriting tasks by generating personalized email content tailored to the prospect's industry, role, and pain points. They can create industry-specific examples for relevant and persuasive content. Plus, they can create multiple versions of the same email for A/B testing, and even help with automating follow-up emails to ensure consistent communication with prospects.

Additionally, LLMs excel at identifying patterns in massive data sets. This can help sales reps identify trends in prospect behavior or see correlations between customer needs and preferences.

By feeding LLMs information about the target audience, autonomous AI agents can generate detailed and accurate B2B buyer personas. With these resources, sales reps can tailor their messaging and outreach strategies more effectively.

Overall, LLM-powered AI agents have the potential to revolutionize the sales landscape and improve efficiency across the board. With these tools, sales reps can make the most of their valuable time. They can focus on more strategic tasks, such as managing and training their team of AI agents.

With the right guidance and best practices in place, SDRs can become managers overseeing a team of AI agents, streamlining sales processes, and increasing productivity. The future of sales is exciting, and LLMs are at the forefront of this transformation.

Prompting ChatGPT: Using AI in the Sales Cycle

> *"I'd be more worried about being replaced by another salesperson who is empowered by intelligence than by a machine." – Peter Schwartz*

> *"AI just scales processes and abilities. Augment a flawed process run by a subpar SDR - you'll blow up." – Florian Decludt*

At first GPT (Generative AI, whatever you want to call it in any productized flavor: ChatGPT, LLaMA, Claude, Bard) looked to me just like any other hype bubble. It generated the same rapid excitement as NFTs, VR helmets, and even the metaverse. Perhaps you saw it the same way.

But the reality is that it can be a useful tool, and it's quickly becoming a part of the fundamental sales, marketing, and customer relationship journey we can no longer ignore.

However, at its core, GPT is like an ambitious intern waiting to learn. While it holds near-unlimited potential, rest assured prompting it is a skill, and synergizing with it is up to you. Prompt Engineer positions often don't even require a technical background and can pay $375K per year. For now, your focus should be on nourishing and feeding it with the right information.

Prompts may be fast and flashy but the data is often off-kilter so stay paranoid to protect your reputation. (Remember that attorney that submitted bogus case law hallucinated by ChatGPT? Ouch!)

That's why I'm working steadfastly with engineers and product people across the globe to prompt GPT in an ever more sophisticated manner. My goal is for ChatGPT to apply the heuristics that guide my human sales processes as much as possible. If you've experimented with ChatGPT, you'll know that's easier said than done. Humans excel in reasoning, tailoring, and customization – what I call advanced synthesis or personalization stacking.

I'm not sure any big data crunching algorithms or LLMs can synthesize these abilities at our level – yet.

How can a machine challenge you? Push back? Reframe your thinking? How can it understand communicating boldly, with gravitas, poise, and insight? Can you program it to display empathy? It's a brave new world. At the same time, even though I think we're a long way off from ChatGPT writing high-quality sales messaging, there's still a place for AI in the sales space.

I believe OpenAI and GPT will be leveraged mainly for seller augmentation rather than replacement.

((Of course, some companies take the other view. Innovative startups are

already trying to supplant their entire top funnel with autonomous sequencing. At this writing, CIENCE 2.0 is even live with full omnichannel outbound including AI/NLP-driven cold calling. I'm authorized to share a sample call.))

Let me hand you back to David Youngblood, for a moment:

David is a seasoned sales veteran, entrepreneur, and GTM strategist with a "very particular set of skills, skills he has acquired over a very long career," (Liam Neeson style.) Not only is David well-traveled and a polyglot, but he also possesses a unique talent for engaging in dialogue with AI across various Generative AI platforms, including GPT, Midjourney, and many others.

David's expertise lies in developing and implementing innovative techniques that push the boundaries of AI, consistently challenging it to exceed expectations. Here's what he has to say about GPT in sales.

The Dawn of AI in B2B Sales

The advent of AI has brought about a paradigm shift in various industries, and sales is no exception. AI, in the form of GPT and LLMs, is not just a buzzword but a powerful tool that's quickly becoming an integral part of the sales journey.

GPT and LLMs, with their ability to understand and generate human-like text, are transforming the way sales professionals interact with prospects and customers. They are like interns, eager to learn and adapt, and with the right training, they can significantly augment a salesperson's capabilities.

The Art of Prompting GPT and LLMs: Unlocking the AI Vault

Imagine you're a skilled locksmith, standing before a grand vault filled with the treasures of AI. This vault, represented by GPT or other Large Language Models (LLMs), has an extraordinary ability to unlock a wealth of insights, but it needs the right key from you to open. That's what prompting these AI models is like - a quest where you're crafting the perfect key, and the AI is revealing the treasures within.

Prompting GPT and LLMs isn't just about turning the key; it's an art form that requires a deep understanding of your vault. You need to know its mechanisms, its quirks, and how it responds to your key. The goal is to craft the perfect key that unlocks the desired output, much like a locksmith crafting a key to open a particular lock.

Creating effective prompts is like crafting the perfect key. Your prompts need to be precise and engaging, guiding the AI in the right direction without overwhelming it with too many instructions at once. They also need to be engaging, sparking the AI's 'creativity' and encouraging it to reveal interesting and valuable responses.

But here's the thing: AI, like a vault, is following your key, but it's not truly thinking. It's matching probabilities, predicting the next word or sentence based on the shape of the key you've given it so far. When it completes the next word or sentence, it's choosing the most likely outcome based on the context of the information you've shared.

That's why it's so crucial to craft the right prompts. Using short, declarative sentences and sequential steps can help guide the AI to provide answers that are closer to your needs. It's like crafting a key with the right cuts and grooves, helping the vault understand the shape and direction of the key.

So, the next time you're prompting GPT or another LLM, remember: you're not just turning a key. You're a locksmith, crafting the perfect key to unlock the vast treasures of AI. The clearer and more engaging your key, the better your vault will be able to follow your lead and reveal a wealth of insights that meet your needs. So, take a deep breath, step up to the vault, and unlock the incredible potential of language generation.

Actually Leveraging AI in the Sales Cycle

Artificial Intelligence (AI) is a transformative tool that can be integrated at various stages of the sales cycle, acting as a trusted sidekick to sales professionals. Here's a breakdown of how AI can be a game-changer at each stage so read on and let's try out some prompts:

LEAD GENERATION:

The process begins, as it always does, with identifying potential customers or leads. AI simplifies this step by sifting through enormous data to pinpoint patterns and forecast which prospects might convert into customers.

By delving into a prospect's online behavior, social media activity, and other data points, AI gauges their potential interest in your offerings. This is where the prowess of a Business Data Aggregator comes into play, offering precise B2B contact and company insights to propel organizational growth. For example, a software company might use AI to analyze the online behavior of potential leads, identifying those who have visited their website multiple times or engaged with their content on social media, indicating a potential interest in their product.

Sample prompt: "Utilizing all available information from our CRM and Business Data Aggregator, please create a list of the top target accounts most likely to convert based on their engagement, for my territory, that haven't yet purchased from us."

CRAFTING PERSONALIZED OUTREACH:

With leads in the pipeline, it's time to initiate a conversation. AI aids in devising personalized cold emails that resonate with each prospect's unique interests and requirements. By dissecting data about each lead, AI ensures your emails not only capture attention but also strike a chord. AI empowered Sales Engagement Platforms are instrumental here, fine-tuning email content and optimizing delivery timings.

Sample prompt: "Please write a tailored step-1 Cold-Email to 'Amelia Smith' about the 'New Product Line.' Then, add her to the automated workflow for that sequence. Reference any relevant insights from our LinkedIn integration when personalizing communications."

LEAD PRIORITIZATION:

Not all leads are created equal. While some show promise, others might not be the right fit. AI is adept at evaluating and ranking leads, ensuring sales professionals invest their time wisely. By assessing factors like a lead's interaction with your content, AI gauges their interest and potential worth.

A sales team could use AI to prioritize leads who have engaged with their emails or website multiple times, indicating a higher level of interest in their product. Predictive Analytics platforms are the unsung heroes here, scoring leads based on their propensity to convert.

Sample prompt: "Utilizing all available information from our CRM and Predictive Analytics, please create a list of the top target existing contacts, that have a cross-sell or upsell opportunity, most likely to convert based on scoring, and adjusting for a heavier weight for those contacts that have previously engaged."

TACKLING BUYER HESITATIONS:

Sales isn't always smooth sailing. Buyer hesitations and objections are par for the course. For instance, if a sales professional frequently encounters objections about price, AI could analyze past interactions to identify the most effective responses to this objection.

AI steps in by offering insights into prevalent concerns and suggesting effective rebuttals. By studying past sales dialogues, AI pinpoints recurring objections and offers strategies to navigate them. This is where Conversation Intelligence Platforms shine, dissecting sales interactions to enhance future conversations.

Sample prompt: "Based on all available CRM, Predictive Analytics, Data Aggregation, and historical correspondence with this company and their 'buying committee,' as compared to historical sales cycles when objections regarding price came up, for 'look-alike' companies, what would the best action plan and messaging be to solve for overcoming those objections, proactively?"

Building Lasting Client Relationships:

Beyond the sale, AI plays a pivotal role in nurturing enduring client relationships. By analyzing client data, AI offers insights into their preferences, enabling sales professionals to tailor their interactions. Moreover, AI takes over mundane tasks like sending follow-up emails, allowing sales teams to concentrate on deepening client relationships.

Marketing Automation Platforms are invaluable here, automating tasks based on client behavior. For example, after a successful sales call, AI could automatically send a follow-up email to the client, providing additional information about the product and next steps.

Sample prompt: "After sending this 'email,' assign the prospect to the appropriate sequence or nurture campaign, then, create a task for me to follow up in X days, put it on my Calendar and duplicate the task in my CRM."

NAILING THE PRODUCT DEMO:

The product demo is the grand finale. AI ensures it's a hit by offering insights into what clicks with the audience. By evaluating past demos and gathering customer feedback, AI recommends presentation strategies that captivate and convince. Sales Enablement Platforms are the maestros here, guiding on the most impactful content and demo strategies. For example, if past demos that included a live product walkthrough were more successful, AI could suggest including this element in future demos.

Sample prompt: "Please review the historical communications and correspondence with this company and its contacts, and compare the conversations with those that are from look-alike companies, where the deals were converted to 'WON,' then, analyze and compare to solve for creating a list of content suggestions and key points that would yield the highest probability of converting the deal."

Remember, while AI is a formidable force, it's the human element that seals the deal. AI is a tool, enhancing human capabilities, offering insights, and automating mundane tasks. But the final handshake? That's all human.

STORYTIME: SARAH'S AI-ENHANCED SALES JOURNEY...

In the bustling city of Silicon Heights, Sarah, a spirited sales professional at TechBoost, is on a mission. With the company's latest software solution, she's determined to make a mark in the B2B space.

One morning, while sipping her latte, Sarah uses the Business Data Aggregator. "It's like having a detective on my team," she muses, watching the AI sift through data, identifying potential leads.

Spotting FutureCorp as a promising lead, Sarah crafts an email using the Sales Engagement Platform. "Dear FutureCorp," she types, then, the AI fills in the rest based on CRM data, "Given your recent endeavors in digital transformation, our solution might be the missing piece in your puzzle."

Intrigued, FutureCorp responds. Sarah, relying on the Predictive Analytics Software, notes, "They're not just interested; they're eager. This could be big."

As conversations progress, FutureCorp voices some concerns. Sarah, ever-prepared, turns to the Conversation Intelligence Platform. "Last time a client had similar concerns," she recalls, "the AI suggested a strategy that turned the tables."

With the relationship strengthening, Sarah leans on her Marketing Automation Platform. "It's like having a personal secretary," she smiles, as the AI schedules follow-up emails, ensuring FutureCorp feels valued.

The D-Day arrives: the product demo. Sarah, armed with insights from the AI Supercharged Tech-Stack, delivers a presentation that leaves FutureCorp spellbound.

Weeks later, as Sarah hangs up after a successful deal closure with FutureCorp, she reflects, "The AI was my compass, guiding me through. But the journey, the relationship, the trust? That was all... us."

This tale exemplifies the harmony of AI and human touch in the sales cycle, each amplifying the other, leading to triumphant outcomes.

Decoding AI Prompt Design: Your Essential Guide

The right prompts can transform the capabilities of AI models, and the wrong ones can leave you screaming at your device. Whether you're an AI veteran or a newcomer, mastering the sequence of operations in prompt design can significantly elevate your AI interactions.

We've already discussed prompts a lot in this book, but there are still some additional insights to share.

Key Terms - Prompt Order of Operations: Each term is a potential 'Prompt Field.' (Yep, that acronym is "Poo."- You read that right.)

As you're prompting, there are a variety of 'Prompt Fields' you can utilize to steer, or guide your outcomes with LLMs. It's important to be mindful of all of the potential variables and know what the capacity and limitations are of your environment.

There's certainly too much, but also too little, in terms of 'context' that the AI uses to respond to your prompt. Below, we cover many, not all, of 'Prompt Fields' you can utilize for instruction while maximizing your output from LLM's and Generative AI's.

ROLE: Define the Role - Specify the desired perspective or expertise for the AI model to utilize in response to your prompt.

Examples:

1. Role: Medical Professional

2. Role: Customer Support Representative

3. Role: Financial Analyst

Use Case: For instance, if you're creating a prompt to generate a medical diagnosis, you might specify the role as "Medical Professional." This guides the AI to respond with the expertise and perspective of a healthcare provider.

TASK: Clearly State the Task - Define the specific task or request to be performed by the AI model.

Examples:

1. Task: Provide a diagnosis based on patient symptoms.

2. Task: Generate a response to customer inquiries regarding product features.

3. Task: Analyze financial data and generate a forecast for the next quarter.

Use Case: If you're looking for a detailed financial analysis, you could state the task as "Analyze financial data and generate a forecast for the next quarter." [This clearly communicates what you want the AI to accomplish.]

FORMAT: Specify the Desired Format - Define the format of the desired output, such as a structured document or specific file type.

Examples:

1. Format: Table

2. Format: Code

3. Format: Plain Text

Use Case: If you need the output in a structured document, you could specify the format as "Table." This ensures the AI's response aligns with your desired presentation style.

TERMS (AND/OR) DEFINITION(S): Provide a Concise Definition of Key Terms - Offer a clear and concise definition or explanation of the key terms or concepts in the prompt.

Examples:

1. Term: Artificial Intelligence (AI)

Definition: The simulation of human intelligence in machines that are programmed to think and learn like humans.

2. Term: Machine Learning

Definition: A subset of AI that uses statistical techniques to enable computer systems to learn from data without being explicitly programmed.

3. Term: Natural Language Processing (NLP)

Definition: The ability of a computer program to understand and interpret human language in a valuable way.

Use Case: If your prompt involves complex, uncommon, unique or technical terms, providing definitions can help the AI understand and use these terms correctly. For example, defining "Machine Learning" can be crucial when asking the AI to explain this concept.

CONTEXT: Offer Detailed Description(s) - Provide a comprehensive description or context for the prompt.

Examples:

1. Description: Use Case in Customer Service, Context: The results are intended to generate responses for customer inquiries related to product features, troubleshooting, and order status.

2. Description: Use Case in Legal Research, Context: The results would be designed to generate legal opinions and analysis based on a given set of facts and relevant case law.

3. Description: Use Case in Financial Analysis, Context: The result aims to generate financial forecasts and investment recommendations based on historical data and market trends.

Use Case: Providing a detailed context, such as "Use Case in Legal Research," helps the AI understand the scenario in which the prompt is being used, allowing it to generate more accurate and relevant responses.

EXAMPLE(S): Include an Example - Illustrate the desired output by providing an example.

Examples:

1. Use Case: Requesting a code snippet in the response.

Example:

"class HelloWorld {

* public static void main(String[] args) {*

*   System.out.println("Hello World!");*

*   // Hello World!*

* }*

}"

2. Use Case: Responding with a recommendation.

Example: "Recommendation: For optimal performance when writing prompts, use an example."

3. Use Case: Creating a prompt for Midjourney.

Example: "/imagine prompt: A stunning Halo Reach landscape with a Spartan on a hilltop, lush green forests surround them, clear sky, distant city view, focusing on the Spartan's majestic pose, intricate armor, and weapons, Artwork, oil painting on canvas, --ar 16:9"

Use Case: Including an example, like "What are the symptoms and treatment options for COVID-19?" gives the AI a clear idea of the type of response you're looking for.

INSTRUCTION(S): Provide Specific Instructions - Give clear and specific instructions or guidelines for creating the prompt.

Examples:

1. Instruction: "Include a summary of the patient's medical history and current symptoms."

2. Instruction: "Write your response in [LANGUAGE]."

3. Instruction: "Include any and all available relevant reference materials or content."

Use Case: Providing specific instructions, such as "Include a summary of the patient's medical history and current symptoms," helps guide the AI's response to meet your specific needs.

TONE: Specify the Desired Tone - Define the desired tone or style for the AI model's response.

Examples:

1. Tone: Formal and Informative

2. Tone: Casual and Conversational

3. Tone: Authoritative and Persuasive

Use Case: Specifying the desired tone, like "Formal and Informative," guides the AI to respond in a manner that aligns with your communication style or the situation's requirements.

INTENTION: State the Intention - Describe the intended outcome of the prompt, including relevant use cases or context. Think of it as, *"If this prompt is successful, it would yield these as the results."* ('Objective' is also effective.)

Examples:

1. Intention: Generating a comprehensive medical report to assist healthcare professionals in diagnosing patients accurately.

2. Intention: Providing customers with detailed information about the product to support their purchasing decisions.

3. Intention: Assisting financial analysts in making informed investment decisions based on accurate and reliable forecasts.

Use Case: Stating the intention, such as "Generate a comprehensive medical report to assist healthcare professionals in diagnosing patients accurately," helps the AI understand the desired outcome of the prompt.

COMPARE ALTERNATIVE TECHNIQUES: As a prompter, compare the prompt instructions with alternative approaches to prompt design, considering their pros and cons. You can even ask the LLM to attempt multiple techniques in their response so you can assess.

Examples:

1. Technique Comparison: Using a rule-based system vs. employing a machine learning model for diagnosing diseases.

2. Technique Comparison: Keyword matching vs. sentiment analysis for identifying customer sentiment in social media posts.

3. Technique Comparison: Using Chain or 'Tree of Thought' vs. deep learning models for predicting stock market trends.

Use Case: Comparing the prompt terms with alternative approaches can help you understand the pros and cons of different strategies being utilized by the AI to enhance and refine future prompting.

DEFINE EVALUATION METRICS: Instruct the LLM to identify and use appropriate metrics to assess their performance and user satisfaction of the prompt. You can try asking it to score and/or grade in a variety of ways.

Examples:

1. Evaluation Metric: Accuracy - Measure the correctness of generated diagnoses compared to ground truth data.

2. Evaluation Metric: Usefulness - Evaluate the prompt's efficiency in providing useful and thorough responses.

3. Evaluation Metric: Customer Satisfaction Score - Assess user feedback and satisfaction with the generated customer service responses as it relates to your role as a [ROLE]. Grade on a scale value of 100.

Use Case: Identifying metrics like "Accuracy" or "Usefulness" allows you to assess the performance of the AI's responses and make necessary adjustments.

SELF-AUDIT and/or VALUATION: Implement and incorporate self-auditing, self-limiting, and self-validating mechanisms to ensure responsible utilization of AI models.

Examples:

1. Mechanism: Bias Detection - Assess your prompt outputs for biases and take corrective actions.

2. Mechanism: Input Validation - Verify the input data to ensure it aligns with the expected outputs format and range.

3. Mechanism: Compliance Checks - Implement checks to ensure the generated responses are factual and comply with relevant laws and regulations.

Use Case: Implementing mechanisms like "Bias Detection" or "Input Validation" ensures responsible utilization of AI models and maintains the quality of the AI's responses.

PERFORMANCE OPTIMIZATION: Optimize Performance - Apply techniques to optimize prompt system performance, such as caching frequently used prompts and reducing resource consumption.

Examples:

1. Technique: Prompt Indexing - Store frequently used terms in contextual reference memory to utilize as a context source for future prompts. (This instructs the LLM to easily scan and recall an index source, specifically and typically limited to that specific chat session.)

2. Technique: Model Pruning - Remove unnecessary context or parameters from the prompt to reduce memory and processing footprint and resource requirements.

3. Technique: Batch Processing - Process multiple prompts simultaneously to improve overall efficiency and output. (This can help maximize token utilization, and time for the user.)

Use Case: Techniques like "Prompt Caching" or "Model Pruning" can improve the efficiency and performance of the AI system, reducing token use among other things.

DOCUMENTATION: Document Results - Thoroughly document the results and outcomes of prompt design experiments and implementations. Provide a written iteration of a prompt template that could be used to recreate your result utilizing all relevant criteria.

Examples:

1. Master Prompt Template: [Prompt Template Name]
2. Role: [Specify Role]
3. Task: [Specify Task]
4. Format: [Specify Format]
5. Terms and/or Definition(s): [Specify Definitions]
6. Context: [Specify Context]
7. Example Prompt: [Specify Example Prompt]
8. Instructions: [Specify Instructions]
9. Tone: [Specify Tone]
10. Intention: [Specify Intention]
11. Compare Alternative Techniques: [Specify Comparison]
12. Evaluation Metrics: [Specify Metrics]
13. Self-Auditing and Validation: [Specify Mechanisms]
14. Performance Optimization: [Specify Techniques]
15. Documentation: [Specify Documentation Details]
16. Disclaimers: [Specify Disclaimers]
17. Continuous Improvement: [Specify Improvement Strategies]

Use Case: Thoroughly documenting the results and outcomes of your prompts helps you track your progress and make improvements over time.

DISCLAIMERS: Include Disclaimers - Instruct the LLM to consider necessary disclaimers to clarify the limitations and potential risks associated with the prompt output or request.

Examples:

1. Disclaimer: The generated diagnosis should not substitute professional medical advice.

2. Disclaimer: The provided product information is subject to change without notice. Please verify with the official sources.

3. Disclaimer: The financial forecasts are based on historical data and market trends and may not guarantee future results.

Use Case: Including disclaimers, such as "The generated diagnosis should not substitute professional medical advice," helps clarify the limitations and potential risks associated with the AI's responses.

IMPROVEMENT: Continuously Improve - Embrace a mindset of continuous improvement, staying updated with the latest research, user feedback, and industry trends to refine and optimize prompt design. Assign 'Improvement' as a suggestion in the response from your prompt. (Only applicable for LLMs with web access)

Examples:

1. Improvement Strategy: Regularly review and incorporate new medical research findings into the prompt for accurate diagnosis.

2. Improvement Strategy: Gather and analyze customer feedback to identify areas of improvement in all prompt responses. (For use in an integrated tech-stack business environment.)

3. Improvement Strategy: Stay updated with financial market trends and adjust your response's forecasting techniques accordingly.

Use Case: Embracing a mindset of continuous improvement, like regularly reviewing and incorporating new [prompt context] into the prompt, ensures your AI interactions stay relevant and effective.

In review here, Prompt Order of Operations (POO) serves as your comprehensive guide to unlocking the power of AI through effective prompt design. It demystifies the complexities of AI interactions, providing you with practical knowledge and tools to navigate this dynamic field. Remember, the journey of AI is one of continuous learning and improvement, and with this guide, you're well-equipped to embark on this exciting journey.

Embracing the AI Revolution in Sales

Effectively prompting these AI models is akin to learning a new language, one that allows us to converse with these digital entities. It's a language of clarity, precision, and engagement. And as we become more fluent, we unlock the potential to transform our sales processes, making them more efficient, more targeted, and ultimately, more successful.

But remember, AI isn't a magic key that instantly unlocks all our sales challenges. It's a tool, a powerful one, but a tool nonetheless. It's there to augment our capabilities, not replace them. It's there to take on the heavy lifting, allowing us to focus on what we humans do best - building relationships, understanding complex emotions, and making strategic decisions.

So, as we stand on the brink of this AI revolution in sales, let's not be daunted. Instead, let's embrace the opportunity to learn, adapt, and grow. Let's leverage AI to enhance our sales prowess, drive more sales, and ultimately, achieve our goals.

Chapter 5: Deeper Magic

"The world is full of magic things, patiently waiting for our senses to grow sharper." – W.B. Yeats

Pareto your life. The 80/20 rule dominates everything. Time is our most precious asset. We all have the same 24 hours in a given day. Unfortunately, 80% of your day is wasted time. When you realize this, you assess where you win (not lose) to understand your most effective actions.

Tim Ferriss was heavily influenced by Richard Koch of *The 80/20 Principle*, that blue and yellow masterpiece by a South African ex BCG and Bain consultant that made a killing on Betfair using his "star principle" to invest in the absolute leader of a niche. Everyone that I coach reads Koch first. And we see the power law everywhere in sales. Jim Holden posits that 80% of sellers "service demand" but only 20% "create demand." I do believe that's true so choose your camp.

Which one are you? Sand in the jar first or the big rocks?

"Do two things that scare you by lunch" is a motto I learned from my grandfather. He was a World War II bomber pilot with no degree that became a real estate mogul. He built up and sold an electronics company to the Chinese and died with 35 million in wealth that he gave to mental health charities. I once drove to Palm Desert and asked him what the secret was to his success, "If

I don't get one or two major things done by lunch, it isn't worth working."

He never retired and still did this till he was 92.

The point is if you focus reactively on putting the sand into the jar – the starred emails, the internal meetings, or getting to inbox zero – you'll miss your chance to take those big shots. Find the big rocks; the things that scare you and knock those out first. I'm talking about things like: calling a CEO, VC or Board member.

If you're looking at something and it makes you nervous or gives you butterflies, "feel the fear and do it anyway," like Jack Canfield loves to say.

The other huge reason Pareto is so important is that the JMM is all about actioning on leading indicators vs. the lagging indicators like CRM KPIs (h/t Jason Jordan and *4 Disciplines of Execution* - 4DX - by Sean Covey). We must develop a radical and proactive bias for action, and be efficient in execution of *smart* daily activity.

It's all about the "List." Keep that list simple. That's the best way I've found to live the 80/20 principle and stay organized while prospecting on a daily basis. Constantly make and stack rank lists. Stack rank it, color code it, and drip to it.

You also need a list of everyone you've ever talked with or who's expressed interest so you can nail follow up.

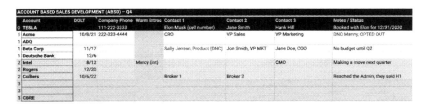

Account	DOLT	Company Phone	Warm Intros	Contact 1	Contact 2	Contact 3	Notes / Status
TESLA		111-222-3333		Elon Musk (cell number)	Jane Smith	Hank Hill	Booked with Elon for 12/31/2020
Acme	10/8/21	222-333-4444		CRO	VP Sales	VP Marketing	DNC Manny, OPTED OUT
ADQ							
Beta Corp	11/17			Sally Jensen, Product (DNC)	Jon Smith, VP MKT	Jane Doe, COO	No budget until Q2
Deutsche Bank	12/6						
Intel	8/12		Mercy (int)			CMO	Making a move next quarter
Rogers	12/20						
Colliers	10/6/22			Broker 1	Broker 2		Reached the Admin, they said H1
CBRE							

ABSD Sales Tracker

That's why I developed the color-coded and stack-ranked ABSD (Account-Based Sales Development) Tracker to get your time back. I set world records with this simple stack-ranked tracker in Google Sheets. Get in touch - happy to share it with you! You can put it into Trello, Asana, Monday.com, Salesforce Kanban view, Highrise, Miro - you name it. How it looks is not important, it's what it does to make you wildly efficient immediately.

You can get a free download of the ABSD Tracker template by going to SalesSuperpowers.com/bonus.

Dress it up or down however you like. Use it right, and you can get an 8-hour day done in 1.6 hours. Every week reach out and nurture your Priority 1s walking them up a ladder of engagement.

The idea is to foster a constant obsession with INTERACTIVITY as the key currency of a healthy outbound campaign. Figure out which of your 200 accounts per quarter are the ones and twos interacting with you the most. Here's how you use numbers to stack rank:

- "0" means you closed the deal or had a meeting
- "1" means it's scalding hot / they're responding
- "2" means there are signs of life: signals like profile views or high opens
- "3" is greenfield: no reaction yet

Read *The 80/20 Principle* by Richard Koch and apply it as an overlay to ideas like *10X Rule* and *Fanatical Prospecting* to achieve orders of magnitude more output. Genius synthesized!

Beware: after pursuing about 150 prospects, your brain just goes fuzzy.

This brain fog has been proven by genuine scientific study. It's called the Dunbar number, and comes from studying primate societies and the number of nodes in the neocortex.

You can make a stack ranked list in any medium, but you've got to be leveraging it daily, even hourly: ranking, re-ranking, and stack-ranking the priority of who you are going after to unlock the greatest power law in the universe - like gravity. The power law of distribution is inexorable, it must work in any system. Ignore it or violate it at your peril. If this is all you get from this book, it's worth a million dollars.

This basic process alone will give you so much leverage. It helped me set world records in mobile marketing prospecting back in a time when most of the tech tools salespeople use today to automate simply didn't exist.

Nurture your #1s walking them up a "ladder of engagement" with enablement content. Some top reps even build their own private newsletter for just their warmest clients. Whenever you share an article or content with warmer prospects, remember "add commentary to curation."

In other words, don't just share the link, say something like, "My opinion on this topic is..." or if you share a white paper, "Here's the point that I think would be most relevant to you." Your voice transposed over your brand's voice creates a powerful synthesis that gets noticed.

Networked intelligence forms the bedrock foundation for Reid Hoffman's entire premise of LinkedIn. Utilizing 2nd degree open profiles, you can filter through a node like a famous thought leader by selecting "connections of name" in a LinkedIn Sales Navigator (Nav) search. Teamlink is extremely powerful too, but nobody really uses it. So you should! The ability to see if anyone in your company is connected to a prospect so you can ask for a warm intro. Ghostwriting a note to get a warm referral is as powerful and rare as a handwritten note.

"Jane, if you are well connected to Jim, can you please send along this note:

Hey Jim – Based on how we help X, Y, Z company do <really awesome thing>, we could be doing a lot with {Your.Co}. up for a chat?"

Follow the spear format (hyper-short - no paragraphs). Relentlessly call up and down the org chart via switchboard to get internal referrals so you can name-drop and add hidden info not found on LinkedIn or Google to personalize your outreach. Keep track of extension numbers per contact, for faster access on your 4th and 5th attempt.

Remember, hidden info isn't always "confidential," it could be political or sensitive in nature - like a vendor will be cut, or someone's about to be fired or promoted.

Story time: I was sitting in Chinatown one day and needed to get into Best Buy mobile. I noticed that an engineer on our team used to work there. I shot him a note on our internal Slack; he sent a message to his former colleague on Facebook and invited her to lunch at our Seattle HQ that day!

This means in a matter of minutes using Teamlink, LinkedIn, Facebook and networked intelligence, I unlocked a senior mobile product manager meeting in near real-time. Are you actually checking and using all your teamlinks? Are you taking time to ghostwrite warm intros? Make it easy for your network to refer you.

Many sellers have a weird patch where they don't have any single 2nd degree intros to access. But others have a very big network in one niche. That's why it paid off for me to stay in Mobile Marketing for 14 years. If you have a significant niche network, you've got plenty of introduction inroads. You'll notice the ABSD tracker has a column just for mapping warm intros either via your 1st degree or 2nd degree teamlinks. Take the time to do this. Also map pathways into accounts via your own C-Levels and even VC network.

Are you co-selling with affiliated sellers who sell SaaS tech in adjacent spaces? This 'better together' story is powerful - using automation like Crossbeam or Reveal to open up the partner-channel ecosystem driven sale instantaneously on integration. I trust Blake Williams for advice here. But many sales leaders don't realize they can unlock it themselves or work with their Head of Channel (and partners') to quickly compare notes and gain powerful, immediate intel/intros.

One of my best stories in this area took place from Atlanta all the way to England on a quiet country lane. Our Director of Channel Partnerships went to Cambridge with the CMO of one of the largest cable companies in the US. They even played rugby together in secondary school. Their parents still lived side by side as neighbors back in Cambridge. That opened the deal and ultimately closed it. The "know, like and trust factor" ran so deep it spanned oceans and a lifetime.

Get all your accounts into a stack-ranked tracker. Make sure you map the DOLT: date of last touch, and be diligent about following up. Always complete the "next steps" field because your CRO will love you. Additionally, get the Sales Navigator mobile app and save every key account and contact you can think of to start monitoring that custom feed for trigger events.

Clear Nav now and reload just the perfect accounts and contacts to curate a custom stream. Then you can leverage every relevant update as an impetus to comment, reach out or customize a touch point. When you are searching for key prospects, look for the company name from standard LinkedIn and click on "people," then go to "decision makers" to let LinkedIn show you via its algorithm who it sees as the DMs in your account. Then save them to track and interact in Nav.

Here are a few additional concepts I learned from Tim Ferriss over the years, which save a lot of time:

First, start time blocking your calendar not just for phone prospecting but for real-time "client conversations." Literally, block out time to have real-time chats. Speak to people now - what are you waiting for?

You'll also want to leverage batching and monotasking. Instead of coming to work and chipping away at "Inbox Zero," spend the first 45 minutes doing the first prong of your TRIPLEs (dropping VMs). You can email them later, or they're likely already running in an active sequence. Pick set times to batch your tasks into a group and knock them out one by one.

The "one by one" part is crucial here. Monotask. Don't multitask. The brain cannot handle multitasking; it vastly limits productivity and creativity.

Another prime example of monotasking is when you're calling a long list of phone numbers, drop any bad number immediately and just TRIPLE on working numbers. It takes 2-3 minutes per number to rifle through databases and find an accurate record. Risk 10 of those and you've blown through 20-30 min of a precious call block in the golden hours. That's why channel-validated data is the holy grail, meaning the list is pre-verified (checked/

called via AI or virtual assistants - VAs), so you know the preference of your prospect ahead of outbounding. (Ask Joey Gilkey, Moaaz Nagori, and Aditya Prakash.)

When I coach people, the first thing I say is: "Show me your calendar." If it's empty of call blocks or chat blocks, I can see instantly why pipeline or client acquisition is anemic. Your income is low as a consequence of inactivity.

Success in sales requires a pale blue collar. Learn to fall in love with the zen of that statement. Chop wood and carry water. You need to carve out time to do prospecting every day. After 20 years, for me, it's become a meditation. It's not just about researching and sending email but unleashing your infinite, childlike sense of wonder and curiosity. People can sense it instantly when we lack compassion and curiosity.

Exercise: Go open your computer now, reach out and touch someone – and move the focus off yourself, and on to *them* in real time.

Time management for full cycle reps is about the Weinberg 3rds: 1/3rd top funnel, one third progression or mid-funnel, and one third closing motions. Therefore, I believe you should prospect against your entire funnel daily including mid-funnel nurture touches like sending books in the mail, cold calling on existing opportunities, and dropping videos/VMs as part of the closing motion.

Prospect your entire funnel.

GPT Lab: Building a daily schedule

GPT is an excellent coach. It can help you optimize your schedule.

Here are three prompts to try:

1. "You are a project manager helping me to create a schedule. Ask me questions like: how many hours do you want to allocate for your daily schedule, and should it include breaks? Based on the response, provide a suggested schedule that incorporates the Pomodoro Technique, three key goals to accomplish, and ensures at least 15 minutes between activities. Ask me when my day starts and when it ends."
2. Generate a detailed plan that spaces out activities by at least 15 minutes and optimizes your focus and productivity."
3. "What are my three most important goals for today? Make sure they are part of the schedule, and write it out as a table with the columns: name, start time, stop time, activity."

The 900 Challenge

"I started reading Justin Michael's methodology from LinkedIn. I downloaded and printed every codex Justin created. I wanted to have it in my hands.

Here's what his methods have done for me:

I entered a new role with no outbound lead gen process in the company. My job was to build out this function, execute it, and teach it to others- essentially, build the plane while flying it. I blew past my lead gen and booked meeting targets for the year, where I was 190% of the goal!

Applying the bump methodology, using the mini case studies, and the triple method were my workhorses for booking meetings.

His teachings have allowed me to build a new outbound system to exceed quota attainment significantly.

I can't speak highly enough of Justin and his method. He has given me the confidence to enter any market, develop a process, generate appointments, and book meetings. Thank you, Justin, your teachings have had a massive impact on my business life, and I'm very grateful."

– Kelvin Vaughan, Vacation Rental Growth Advisor, Vintory

Life is the journey, not the destination. Get addicted to the process and fall in love with client enrollment.

Prospecting is a marathon, not a sprint. So I devised "The Law of 900" – the cumulative impact of prospecting daily is boundless. This is how you truly "unlock unlimited pipeline."

It's like compound interest. It's the gift that keeps on giving.

We brush our teeth daily (mostly) and sleep every day (mainly). We even eat, blink, move, beat our hearts, and breathe every day.

But we procrastinate until "later this week" when prospecting. Then we don't actually do anything. So let's shift our paradigm.

What is the Law of 900?

One day, when I was around 38 years old, I made a personal commitment to prospecting 30 net new strangers per day, every day, for the rest of my life. And guess what? I've kept that commitment for five years.

The results have been wild. Within six weeks, I was generating 6 meetings a day.

By now, I've driven thousands of qualified leads. I no longer consider them prospects, just warm, relevant conversations. From these conversations, deals spring eternal.

But here's the weird thing about conducting an autopsy on those first six meetings:

Meeting #1 was from an InMail sent 3 weeks prior
Meeting #2 sourced from a simple event follow-up
Meeting #3 came from a personalized connection request
Meeting #4 emerged from a post resulting in a random social media interaction

The rest were lucky "thoughts?" bumps on day 2 of a cadence.

Fast forward: I decided to systematize this, and now everyone I coach takes the "900 Challenge."

So, can you contact 30 net new strangers per day, every day, for an entire month? No excuses! Play like a champion. But let's take a look at the fears you might be facing first:

- 1 am? No problem, send 30 InMails.
- Missed your prospecting block? Not to worry, send 30 connection requests.
- Stuck in an airport? Whip out your Sales Nav mobile app and comment intelligently on some prospects' posts
- Don't have Nav? - send custom connects or 1st-degree messages / drop 1st-degree videos (in-app) á la 4th Frame (see book 1: JMM 1.0)

There's always a channel on. There's always a way to prospect effectively - 24/7/365.

The Law of Replenishment / 90-Day Rule echoes the Law of 900. One is biblical, the other a 'Blountism.' I'd wear this on my wrist like an invisible infrared tattoo lighting up as the sun goes down as a constant reminder. A simple sticky note on your laptop will do. ;-)

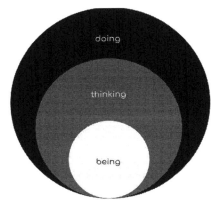

Being – Thinking – Doing

Being influences thinking. Thinking influences doing.

Real evolution means rethinking how you're wired.

The entire performance coaching, sales training, and strategic consulting industry typically falls down because it's obsessed with the fallacy of the outer shell of the diagram: *doing*. Changes outwardly change nothing, aka Einstein's definition of insanity: "doing the same thing over and over again and expecting different results." True transformation comes from assessing your thoughts, self-perception, and your actual "being" (or identity) from which all other elements of "living" radiate and manifest.

According to Joe Dispenza, we run virtually the same mental programs and think the same 70K thoughts every day. Without vastly changing your internal psychology, self-perception, and deeper factors, your life will fall into a karmic cycle, homeostasis, or

Goldilocks Zone. Einstein's definition of insanity is perfect repetition like *Truman Show* meets *Groundhog Day*.

That's where coaching comes in. One deep insight can shift your internal view of yourself and who you are, and from that, an entirely new parallel universe can unfold, creating new perspectives and abilities in an instant. That's why *10X is easier than 2X* (Sullivan/Hardy) because looking at the future in this renaissance way, activates our brain to formulate new neural pathways toward exponential growth, returning us to our native state.

Are you willing to put in the daily work? It can be done in as little as 20 minutes each day just before bed as you're slipping toward unconsciousness in an alpha or theta brainwave state. By changing or "pruning" your thoughts, you visualize new outcomes and replay your day in your mind, revising it as you'd like to have lived. Hat tip Neville Goddard. Note: I always set visualization to sacred music, aka my patented music manifestation process – *Musifestation. (What to listen to? Go to Spotify and type in Solfeggio).*

Legend has it that Salvador Dalí would rest on a metal plate with a key in his hand as he fell toward sleep to awaken the dreamer. If the key fell and clanked, it ensured he stayed slightly awake in that interspace of subconscious peak imagination.

Your vision becomes a self-fulfilling prophecy. But if your actions don't then match your desires, it won't happen for you.

> *"You must get clear for yourself that your only access to impacting life is action." – Werner Erhard*

In my view, humans split into two categories: talkers and doers. My work is for the doers, and I don't know any successful "talkers." Even radio show hosts who talk for a living like Howard Stern and Joe Rogan work their asses off.

So, who's ready to take the challenge and report back in 30 days?

Many of you already have; here's Paul's success story leveraging the JMM in Germany:

"Just closed my highest ever deal with around $100K ARR, cold approached the CMO using JMM. Closed another 250K TCV (3-year contract) last week to secure the second promotion within one year after working with you."

People always ask me for the magic bullet, "JM, how do I personalize this LI message to get a reply?"

Wrong question. Instead ask: "How do I commit to the specific portfolio of daily prospecting actions that will compound and pay off long term?"

Daily prospecting as a lifestyle's cumulative impact and its compound effect cannot be understated. If you take away one thing from this book, it's that. Seven days a week: eat, pray, love, prospect.

Why is a book on prospecting sharing all this life coaching and spiritual advice? Because to find depth and meaning, you must learn to do it in a joyful, heart-centric way. The hustle and grind fall away into a zen practice.

7-Figure Mindset

> *"Be independent of the good opinion of other people."*
> *– Abraham Maslow*

Antifragility is an idea from Nassim Nicholas Taleb. The more challenging a situation gets, the more you adapt to it. Like the pressure creating the diamond, the harder it is, the more valuable the wisdom and lessons you can take away.

How many "No's" can you get per day?

The only reason I'm more successful than you is I get more "No's" than you do.

You can get anyone to say yes if you're willing to hear 1,000 No's. – Byron Katie

Success is an algorithm. It consists of a wide array of constructive actions repeated daily. We need a new mindset for sellers that transcends the comp plan. There is no magic bullet for prospecting. But as you can see, the mindset in this book is an internal operating system by which all the necessary strategies and tactics you could ever need start to flow through you if you think in a certain way.

A lot can be said for identity or "being" radiating at the center before impacting thinking and doing. This is why it's critical to see yourself not just as "the kind of person" capable of earning double or triple your income, but literally "that person." Assume that identity by emanating from that place of infinite truth.

You can't be a 200K earner, hoping, wishing, striving, and struggling to earn 500K, or 1.2MM, one day. Success will be short-lived in that respect and thanks to "hedonic adaptation" you'll sink right back down to previous earnings. Many a lottery winner has ended up bankrupt. Now why is that? With great power comes greater responsibility.

But, you can work with a competent coach like me to unlock your potential.

Understanding elements of your unique genius is practical so that you can double and triple down on them 80/20 Pareto style.

A good coach can unlock shortcuts to catapult you forward. I bring my 20 years of experience to clients to help them crack their problems or realize latent opportunities. We dive far beneath the surface to explore their mindsets impacting thoughts and skill sets.

I opened this section with a quote to stop caring about what other people think about you, because this is the hallmark of self-actualized people. I always joke about going for a "50 under 50" award. All the self-aggrandizing shouting for attention, social media hacking, "personal branding," and beauty pageants got me nowhere.

With a bestseller, 52,000+ followers, 30,000 connections capped, LinkedIn Top Voice recognition, and a rank in the Top 50 in B2B by Lead411, my brand alone has yet to generate a customer or a client from thin air, not once in my 20-year-plus sales career.

LinkedIn fame and connections will add credibility but will not sell for you. You must do this proactively.

It's insane to think people decide like this: "Justin is LinkedIn famous; let's hire him." They only buy from you if they're confident you can produce the result they seek.

So what should you be talking about on your profile?

What you've accomplished for your clients.

Fill your profile with social proof. Use case studies of how you helped similar customers, particularly with statements crafted in their own words. Your customers sell you better than anyone else in the world:

Testimonials make the world go round.

Focus less on building your personal brand, and more on developing relationships with prospects. It's those conversations, those meaningful moments with your prospects, that define whether you'll be an effective salesperson.

When I coach reps, I ask them how many "completes" they had the week before.

Most tell me they've had a meaningful or deep conversation with around 4-5 live human beings at most. You need to double that number.

Put all your focus and energy on one high-quality conversation with a dream prospect, and your sales results will transform. Serve that person powerfully as a trusted advisor. That could even mean you help them with something that isn't even related to your solution. Take those success stories and add them to your profile.

Again, we are only limited by what we believe. That's the mindset we need to master.

"I'm scared to do that. I could never call that person, ask for that, dream that, do that, think that, earn that, and so on. They won't let me do that." Sound familiar?

All these self-limiting beliefs eternally hold us back on this Sisyphean journey up the mountain of life. But it doesn't have to be that way. There is power even in the ASKING for what you truly want, your *Aladdin Factor*, as Jack Canfield calls it. So ASK big!

Jack describes the human psyche by comparing us to a baby elephant tied to a small stake in the ground. When the elephant grows up, it still thinks it's stuck. With a little force, it can break free. It's the perfect metaphor for our self-defined limitations.

This concept speaks to authors that won't write. Dreamers that won't dream. Entrepreneurs that won't launch companies.

Break free from the chains you think are holding you back. "The cave you fear to enter holds the treasure you seek." Joseph Campbell was right; the mantra of this book had a heavy influence on George Lucas.

There are two ways to crack the glass ceiling of your self-imposed limitations:

One, you need to trust your inner voice. Your gut is like a compass leading you to the goals you want to achieve, deep inside.

Two, surround yourself with people who make you better, not just tell you what you want to hear to appease you. But challenge and encourage you to become better. Hear the voices of people who can see your potential without pandering to your ego.

Bonus: Start saying yes to the things you truly fear. Right there, just beyond fear, lies the silver lining, the breakthrough - your limitless pill. Take positive risks. As Jack Canfield always says, "Feel the fear and do it anyway," or the acronym for the illusion of fear: Future Events Appearing Real.

> *"Out of suffering have emerged the strongest souls; the most massive characters are seared with scars." – Khalil Gibran*

Do you want to know the secret to keep prospecting and never burning out?

Prospecting must become as natural as breathing or brushing your teeth. When you want success as much as breathing, you will succeed. You must. It's life or death.

Burn the boats. Commit. Announce your goals. Get a coach or partner, and hold yourself accountable to climb.

Read and re-read this book until you can quote it, until the knowledge seeps out of your pours. I read books 4-5 times and listen to them on Audible applying lessons between sessions.

Even when I was couch surfing in my 20's, had next to nothing, and pretty much walked around 24/7 with an active death wish, I did those basic things that come to us all: sleep, eat, shower, etc.

Prospecting should be as natural, organic, and automatic as blinking to a salesperson.

When you have no choice but to hit your goal, who you are BEING changes. There are no more excuses.

In this book, I'm trying to help you shift WHO you are behind the mask of your mind, thoughts, and identity. These are all illusions, constructs that become excuses.

In my early years, I couldn't deal with my lack of a college degree and used it as an excuse for why I wasn't earning. I forever carried a chip on my shoulder. I've finally put that load down. So should you. We are limited by what we believe.

Once I flipped the script, the eternal sun came out.

My CV drawbacks became my advantages. My lack of college education was an edge in my *Good Will Hunting* story.

My track record driving massive pipelines in 90 days became a worldwide legend in the mobile marketing industry. CEOs used to talk about it on yachts in Cannes. "Should I hire JM?" "That guy's a professional stalker," one replied, "in a good way," he continued. ;-)

All my setbacks allowed me the privilege to grind for 20 years to get real-world experience, and my lack of long tenure made me an expert in developing explosive pipeline in the first 90 days to 6 months. It's now the focus of my practice. I wasn't mired in years of academic study, building on the ideas of those that came before me. I built my system from scratch, for myself, using trial-and-error.

I'm now the world's leading specialist at that niche, and VCs came knocking with millions in 2017 to scale up autonomous prospecting campaigns (by creating an AI model of my brain) to 100 concurrent startups at once, leading to my first book deal.

Fun fact: At this writing, CIENCE is unleashing CIENCE 2.0 AI-Outbound, a fully autonomous soup-to-nuts omnichannel AI for any prospecting workflow. Get ready to jump out of your socks as you hear an AI finally make cold calls and deftly handle customer queries. (I have an authorized recording if you're interested.) Can somebody say "Google Duo?" YouTube it. I've seen platforms like Rightbound.io revolutionize autonomous top funnel, as well, by effectively removing all the pain out of the process: targeting, list building, enrichment, and now…. the outreach slog itself by phone.

If you're terrified to switch companies, switch companies. Are you scared to quit your dead-end job where no one is making a commission? Go elsewhere, or go solo and earn more.

> *"The cave you fear entering contains the treasure you seek."*

I will repeat Joseph Campbell to you, the basis of *Star Wars*. We all remember Luke entering the Dagobah cave where he sees the ghastly apparitions that look so real and cut so deep. Use the force.

The lie you tell yourself is that if you don't work for someone else, you will fail on your own. But Your Name, Inc. will consistently outperform Massive Evil Mega Corp if you go *all in* with the right drive and goals.

As you read this, remember you are as powerful and capable as I am.

Bruce Lee said, "be like water." Water carving rock over thousands of years. Formless. Shapeless. Timeless. With infinite patience and persistence there isn't a single obstacle in this life, you can't conquer. I'm living proof.

You can harness your inner power and focus it like a beam, or you can spray endlessly. Focused power of vision brings about miraculous results. Thank you, Townsend Wardlaw, for this distinction. When you visit with powerful prospects or clients you must own your power. Harnessing that inner confidence can take time but the best way to do it is by knowing and being yourself without expectation.

Who are you being in this moment?

You are an expert at your craft. Your desire to see their business thrive, not just close a deal, must be palpable. Eliminate "commission breath," as Josh Braun loves to say. When I sit with powerful CROs, I relax, take a breath, and look them in the eyes. Focus, be fully there, and listen. Deep listening allows us to find deep insights and sense deeper intent between the words. It allows us to form a spiritual connection even over a zoom. One insight can change a life; create a 1MM dollar ROI – it's truly limitless.

GPT Lab: Reminding yourself you can do it

GPT doesn't tire of reminding you of what you're good at.

Try this prompt:

"As a motivational executive coach, I'd like you to reflect on three greatest strengths or accomplishments. Once you've identified them, consider leveraging these strengths to uplift your mood and boost your motivation.

Additionally, suggest two or three self-care activities or techniques that can help enhance your emotional well-being during challenging times."

New KPIs

KPIs will always be crucial to sales success. We all know that data is the key to consistently improving results. The question is, which KPIs really matter?

I believe we need new key performance indicators (KPIs) to measure "completes per day." What good is cold outreach if hunter reps and SDRs are never having conversations? In my view, a "complete" is either talking live to a prospect or having a direct message (DM) interaction over 2-3 back and forths.

You might get garbage meetings and opportunities that never close if you track them on their own. There needs to be a new calculus around interactivity as the primary metric.

Start to track conversations per day. Real ones. I'm aligned with Joey Gilkey on this one!

In the words of Steve Chandler, "every sale happens in the context of a conversation in the prospect's world." This led me to the creation of my "prospecting richter scale."

PROSPECTING RICHTER SCALE

Face-to-Face = 100X Zoom
Zoom = 10X RT
Real-time DMs = 10X Email
Email = 10X Twitter (X)

To unpack this scale, I need to express the importance of tracking the right metrics from a neuroscience perspective. Let me give you a behind-the-scenes example:

My friend's father has 500MM under management at Oppenheimer, a mutual fund. He never takes a big investment from a new client without first speaking face-to-face looking professional (wearing his best suit and tie), ready to answer all of their toughest questions.

Face-to-face interactions have power - even now in the age of endless forms of digital communication. In fact, in today's world, true human interaction might be more important than ever.

To this day if you break bread with someone, the amount of trust built is orders of magnitude higher than any digital interaction. That's why the "Neighborhood Technique" or "lobby thumping" as my former CEO used to joke, is still sound for business post-pandemic.

Then we go down the scale into Zoom calls – as you'll recall 93% of communication is nonverbal in nature. I have listed DMs as the 3rd rung down in the Prospecting Richter Scale because I truly believe communication is changing. Connection rates are painfully low with cold calls today, and response rates for cold email are dwindling.

Direct message "chat flows" back and forth are quickly becoming a superior signal of interactivity and prospect interest to email replies.

The idea of the above scale is to run your territory with the following prioritization: Get face-to-face as often as you can with prospects. Get them on Zooms, and then into DM chats. If you use cold outreach on LinkedIn and cold email as supplemental to the above powerful form factors the overall outbound prospecting approach will be most effective. It's all neuroscience.

AND NOW TO THE NEW SALES KPIS FOR ALL MANAGEMENT:

Goal = 20 completes per week*
Complete = live interactions w/ prospects
a) live phone call
b) high interaction DMs (over 3 back and forth)

*Note: With a parallel-assisted dialer (PAD) you could even do this per day!

I mentioned before that the silent sales floor is killing business. (Hat tip Tony J. Hughes.) It's not just a lack of prospecting that's causing a problem, but the wrong type of interactions.

Liking, tweeting, sharing, and interacting in endless streams of ads and witty posts, is really NOT building out your book of business. Inspired by Steve Chandler, any time I see a rep that is struggling to hit their number, I pull their calendar for the last week and I judge it by the litmus test of "completes."

Your goal reading this should be to put 10 completes per week, or even 20, onto your calendar immediately. At the end of each week, ask yourself how many "completes" you've actually achieved.

More often than not, salespeople restrict their own success by only interacting with 5 or fewer "live humans." The number of "meaningful interactions" in the sales world is lower than ever. If building relationships is crucial to success in a sales world driven by human psychology, we need to make meaningful connections a priority.

Remember, a "complete" can be a DM interaction that has at least 4 back-and-forths. As valuable as face-to-face interactions are, conversations can still be impactful in other formats. You may even find you encounter some prospects who prefer to communicate through text or video.

Leveraging the right technology can be extremely valuable too. Tools like ConnectAndSell, Salesfinity, Koncert and Orum – parallel assisted dialers – are so incredibly powerful to unlocking new business because they can drive up completions to 20 per day. Because they dial 3 to 10X simultaneously in parallel deftly handling switchboard navigation and hot switching seamlessly and imperceptibly to the answerer. Drop a headcount and over-invest in your list aka "clean data."

Targeting, intent, and triggers trump message-market fit. If you're firing on the wrong people outside the buying window, it's all for naught. Sure, you can trigger a buying window by excavating latent pain to create demand, but you are unlikely to sell to a buyer who just inked a 4-year locked-in SaaS deal. Even if your solution augments. No chance to buy out a contract like that!

SDRs game the metric *meetings per month*. Trish Bertuzzi and Bridge Group surveys benchmarked the median average at 25/

mo and 11 opportunities for high-quality outbound work. But reps can always hit up local "pizza and beer" meet-ups, grab business cards, and inflate their meeting count.

Counsel your sales force that the "purpose of business is to create customers." Even revenue is a lagging indicator as measured in a cracked rearview mirror per Jason Jordan. SDRs should take pride in seeing real partnerships and deal flow come out of their hunting efforts. If they only get a dopamine hit out of banging the gong, they are missing the point that the last 62 meetings they set did not turn into a bonafide customer. Soon SDRs move into an AE role and will respect the quality of good inputs. That's why the JMM is not solely focused on lifting "vanity metrics" like contact rates or open rates. So what if you got a high reply rate when they were all negative? ;-)

Start asking the right questions, such as:

1. What is the caliber of the prospects that ultimately reply?
2. How many actual customers are you creating?
3. What is the quality of those customers even if quantity holds the same?

Old-fashioned KPIs aren't as effective as they once were. We need a new "math of sales" that hinges on smart inputs and outputs. Quality over quantity is a truism because it's another universal law that cannot be violated. How many 3rd party appointment setters have you hired where they generate 15+ meetings for you but you're only happy with 13? See my point?

C-Level Comms

"To be consultative, be assumptive." – Jill Konrath's Paradox

Teaching reps to speak with C-Levels is tricky business. Their main fear/concern is that we will waste their time.

I once called a CRO and asked if it was "Tim Cook." "Of course not!" they replied. Undaunted, I still landed the meeting.

Every bad thing that happens when I'm outbounding, I will turn into a point of leverage. "See every situation from the viewpoint of advantage." That's why I'm so big on humor diffusion as a heuristic for handling objections.

CXOs respond to active listening, curiosity and visuals. You'll never progress a first call to next steps or close a deal if you're not doing the vast majority of the listening.

My #1 goal whenever I hold a Zoom call is to see how much and how deeply I can listen. Be fully there.

Never needy, creepy over-researched personalization. It leaves your CXO prospect wondering: "Why is this vendor trying so hard? They must have something to hide."

Be relevant. Align to their laser-focused priorities which reflect Steve Richard's four demand types:

- Make money
- Save money
- Reduce risk
- Satisfy a government regulation

Once I accidentally called a CEO on his boat after hours...

Friday night... Paradise, the life of a Don Henley lyric. It's about 4pm Pacific and I'm thinking, "I'm running out of daylight to make cold calls." But I have this secret weapon burning a hole in my back pocket.

It's access to ConnectAndSell. So I invite the Salesborgs onto a Zoom call. I've loaded in 200+ VPs of Sales in high tech companies. As an advisor, these are the stunts and opportunities I uniquely get. But instead of hiring somebody else to dial, I do it myself.

The system lights up, I'm chilling in my zen garden. Boom, it's a mistake in the data, instead of a VP it's the CEO.

"Who's this?"

"Justin Michael, OK time?"

"I'm just getting on my boat and the sun is setting."

"Well, I guess the reason for my call is: I'm making this cold call in my backyard, how do I succeed to the level that I end up on a boat on a Friday night instead?"

He chuckled and replied, "Get old!"

"I am old," I admitted. "Just turned 40."

"Really old," he replied sagely and laughed again.

And what proceeded was this beautiful lyrical call in which he lowered the veil on what he was working on. He even identified his Head of Demand Gen as the "CEO of the outbound problem" and was willing to make an immediate introduction.

Next live connect. 4:12 pm.

"Justin, I'm going off-grid – just email me and I'll meet next Wednesday."

To set the stage, I'm holding an exhibition in my Discord group with 20+ people watching including Josh Braun. This guy sets the meeting within 2 hours.

I look down and I've got 2 meetings and a referral in under 15 minutes, twenty Saleborgs as my witness.

Best part is? Remember that CRO on his boat? He writes an email introducing me to his demand gen lead from the bow of his boat during this same call block late Friday evening.

I proudly held up my smartphone to show everyone the proof. I can't even make this stuff up! Truth is stranger than fiction when you unleash your inner honey badger.

So, what actually generated this success? Was it the technology? In part. The technology brought me to the dance. But it didn't bust a rhythm on my behalf. It was the human element that actually made this instantaneous improvisation and success possible. I also didn't handle "I'm on a boat" as an objection; to me is was just a comment because his tone seemed friendly. I read the situation right and scored a key meeting via waterfalling (calling in high to get delegated down).

Here are some big lessons for you to get a meeting with anyone:

- If you're not scared, you have yet to select a target that is valuable enough. I mean it. Aim higher. You need to feel the butterflies.
- Imagine you're them. That's it. Would you respond to your message?
- Think outside of the box. FedEx works. Powerful people will open a FedEx. Imagine if you received a random FedEx not knowing it was from a vendor. What would it need to say to capture and hold your attention? How could it influence you to take a meeting? (Dale Dupree, Stu Heinecke, and Tony Parinello have great ideas here.)
- It's about them. They don't even need to respond. Just keep giving them value. Give them high-utility aka something they can use immediately. Leverage content so good they'd be willing to pay for it.

131

- Don't target people because you're supposed to. If your prospect isn't going to benefit from what you offer, move onto someone else. Get a better patch, even switch companies. Don't sell to people who can't buy.
- Like it or not, society is a caste system and even "flat" startups are bureaucratic. If you can't get a meeting with a VP, go to the CEO, then go to the Board, then go to their VCs. The worst outcome? A VC is so impressed by your grit and tailored value prop for one startup, they introduce you to several other qualified prospects in their portfolio.

"C-Levels speak the language of outcomes and risk," per Tony J. Hughes, and we get "delegated down to whom we sound like." I was shocked in coaching an SDR recently that he had an ultra-low show rate. I asked why he wasn't doing more probing, pain-identification, and peeling of the onion on his initial calls. He responded, "We're not allowed to do any discovery just book the meeting." Ludicrous!

No pain, no sale - remember?

It's critical that you research the business model and craft/understand an effective ROI-based business case before reaching out to the C-Suite. It's imperative to filter through the 10Ks and 10Qs - the annual and quarterly reports - and even several years of these to spot trends in publicly traded companies. (Hat tip Jeff Meyers). Do a Find (Command F) search and find words like "threats" or "weaknesses" in the report.

Having spent thousands of hours directly dialing the cell phones of CXOs, I've encountered a paradox. Most people don't realize that calling high-level people consistently is often easier than trying to master lower-level interactions. They're often nicer, just saying!

Many times you will get an executive assistant. You need to treat gatekeepers like gold and sell to them as if you're speaking directly to the C-Level they screen for. You'll often get put through to a voicemail box and be able to do real damage leaving high-quality personalized voicemails in the manner I've described elsewhere in this book.

Here's a real-world example for you. I was sitting at the LinkedIn office in the Empire State Building one day, working on my target list. I decided to send an InMail to a Board Member from a Japanese conglomerate.

Like butter, he pinged back immediately with his cell phone number. I called him right after that. He answered and arranged a packed board room meeting with his generals back at headquarters to review LinkedIn Sales Navigator, the next week.

What does this tell you? Essentially, you can book an entire onsite C-Suite level meeting, just by being bold enough to simply reach out to a board member.

The natural instinct is to be afraid to reach out to the most powerful people in companies, to think you need to agonize over the perfect messaging for 3 hours, or to feel as if somehow you are unqualified. Remember, their charter is to maximize shareholder value. They want to connect you to the appropriate team so you can help them increase results.

If you have a great solution (which I'm sure you do), boldly believe in it, and interrupt powerful people *boldly* with conviction that you will get deferred to the ultimate decision maker. You can penetrate accounts far faster by aiming above the power line

(Skip Miller) than by trying to endlessly "groundswell" and hoping you'll get introduced to someone's boss. Ain't gonna happen!

Business acumen can be developed very rapidly by reading the *Wall Street Journal*, biographies of famous executives like Larry Ellison and Andy Grove, and spending time in annual reports. Just be curious about how business in general works, read books, blogs or articles about financial literacy and learn how to examine profit & loss (P&L) statements and balance sheets. Marc Periou is someone I suggest you talk with about that – brilliant!

Reps get caught flat-footed thinking, "What on Earth am I even going to talk about with a CEO? That person lives in an alien world to me." But you'll start to see they are ordinary people just like you, they just speak a different language because they are responsible for so many employees' wellbeing. Rather than the megalomaniacal Michael Douglas in Wall Street, they're more like the kind, wise, jovial Oracle in the Matrix. Don't get psyched out – they were once where you are.

Immerse yourself in macro trends, and study how various businesses in their sector work. Watch the stock market, read books by Warren Buffett. It will come together and suddenly, you'll be living in their world, and the talk tracks will just start to click. At Salesforce, they trained us on "speaking CMO." Speaking CXO to me means: understanding financials, public markets, risk and regulation.

You can get a PhD on these topics by taking your CFO/CEO/COO out to lunch or coffee. They are often willing to do this to help you. You can run verbiage by them to see what they'd respond to. Every once in a blue moon a CEO posts on LinkedIn about what they'd actually respond to and it's fascinating: it follows exactly what I've stated above. They hate "generic." Their biggest fear is some vendor "wasting their time." That's why I literally put "I don't want to waste your time" into the top script of all my cold calls if they try to force me to pitch early so they can't deep-six me.

Negging C-Levels

Negging is a term with many bad connotations. But there is value in "challenging" and "pushing back" against your prospect. Be willing to tell the powerful what they *don't* want to hear. Be willing to have bold, even uncomfortable conversations with high-level stakeholders, emphasis on mutual trust and respect. (Ichak Adizes)

Sellers are often so caught up in people-pleasing or thinking that being "nice" is going to get powerful people to do them favors. The truth is, it just lowers your status.

You must get over your "people-pleasing" attempts and become self-actualized. People-pleasing desires come from a little voice in your head that wants to be liked: shut it out.

Heed Maslow's truism: "be independent of the good opinion of others." You can't help a client you're desperately trying to please or worried you'll offend. You can't provide deep insights, deep listening, or high flame coaching. You cannot be afraid of their opinion of you.

Ironically, they'll respect you a whole lot more if you level with them from a place of caring, love and understanding. They may finally have a breakthrough because you told it like it is.

It's worth noting that only one person can maintain alpha status while the other goes beta. Oren Klaff's insights into frames and frame control are important here. In the moment that you are dealing with a CXO as an expert, you have the upper hand from an acumen perspective. Bosworth-style "customer hero stories" are your "get out of jail free card" so you don't get flattened by high-alpha dominant execs.

My ideas about "negging C-levels" come from *The Game* - that controversial Neil Strauss classic so many people are secretly influenced by. It's important to note: he later wrote a book to reverse his thesis and promote monogamy. So, what does "negging" look like from a sales perspective?

It's more subtle than you'd think. If a powerful person responds to your message quickly, answer with:

"Thanks for the prompt response, Name." You slightly check their ego, lowering their status and they have no clue you did it. It insinuates they are lonely or available, with an open calendar. At the very least, always be a peer or business equal.

Remember this stuff can be misconstrued as manipulative and preys on weak egos. Although you can use a million little neg tricks that are psychosociological warfare, there is often collateral damage associated with these grey hat psychosocial techniques. Be subtle and be playful about this rather than cutting someone off at the knees.

Why is it that in dating scenarios we care about "mutuality" but in B2B prospecting "reciprocity" be damned? We cannot take blood from a stone; chemistry must be established at some point or you'll never do a deal much less "get a meeting."

Remember my cardinal rule of B2B integrity. If you simply do what you say, you will separate yourself from 99% of this industry. The world is filled with flakes: don't be one of them! ;-)

GPT Lab: Interview the CEO

Hone your executive conversation skills by roleplaying with GPT.

Here's an example prompt:

"Imagine we're having a casual chat about how I can convince you, as the CEO of a mid-sized software company, to invest in my software with a two-year contract. What are your main concerns and how can I best address them to make you feel confident in the investment? Let's have an informal conversation and not too stuffy. Ask me the first question, and then wait until I respond with [star emoji] to continue."

Anatomy of Earning 7-figures

> *"Everything you've ever wanted is sitting on the other side of fear." – George Addair*

Who you are being, influences how you think, and ultimately what you do.

You will earn high 6 figures or even 7 figures once you shift your fundamental identity and mindset. Trust me on that. You need to change your narrative about yourself from limitation to abundance, from victim to owner. We all have a story, and I'm definitely on my 9th life.

Remember, we are the authors of our own stories.

Despite waiting 2 years to put out *Tech-Powered Sales* because of COVID delays, I built out the *Codices* as temporary training guides for Justin Michael Method (JMM) practitioners as it was developed.

This experimental strategy proved to be a powerful tool. The market validated the discoveries I was making, as reps I coached started landing Fortune 500 meetings within a couple of weeks.

I'd often witness an utterly green seller (maybe a single parent) come out of waiting tables to set appointments with impossible-to-reach C-Levels applying my teachings in mere weeks. It dawned on me that I could train people from all walks of life on my methods and break them down into lucid pedagogy.

I enlisting the feedback of a bright client to bounce ideas off of, a mathematician and teacher, who was working on a garbage truck. No shame in that but Patrick's income tripled overnight, allowing him to purchase a home in Seattle. This gave me tremendous confidence to charge more and eventually codify the entire system to allow for certification. Suddenly I was doing 100K and 200K single days. See how that builds?

That's the secret here. Invest in yourself. Believe in yourself, and keep working.

The more repetitions, the more your confidence will grow in selling, cold calling, and consulting/advising/coaching. Go get in the arena, think fast, break things Zuck-style, and fail forward.

As you grow and get stronger, you will double, triple, and quadruple your earnings. You'll be taxed to death. Trust me, I want you to have this problem. ;-)

Beware the hedonic treadmill where you spend as fast as you earn. Invest in yourself, your personal development, and coaching. Without your health, you have no life. Without giving, it is impossible to receive.

New success equation. Move from:

take -> give

sell -> serve
fear -> gratitude & love
talk -> listen
self-oriented -> selfless (other-oriented)
interesting -> curious
self-promotion -> customer as hero

Abundance solves your financial problem, not over-saving. We reap what we sow. I remember making 310K one year and owing 35K, but there aren't too many problems at $750K+ unless you're a complete fool and blow it on a custom boat, lambos, crypto, and an Instagram life. Health and family must come first. Dedicate yourself to giving all your wisdom away to other people. That's true wealth.

"Give it away now." – Anthony Kedis

It was only when I GAVE instead of taking, SERVED instead of selling, LISTENED instead of talking, CARED instead of ignored, and switched to INTERESTED versus interesting, that everything changed for me.

I have a very thick skull, but when I finally focused on genuinely helping the person in front of me without any need for payback, my life and business finally changed - things got easier, especially around client acquisition and knowing what to do on coaching calls.

I guess I violated the Sandler rule of "seeking fulfillment" in this job. I love what I do, truly. I love helping people, even if I just make their lives 1% better.

You might be wondering, "How can you have a thriving consulting and coaching business if you just give everything away?" It's because all the power is in implementation, customization and the journey you go on to master the psychological operating system behind it.

Earning 7-figures is a profound challenge and accomplishment; I can count my friends on one hand that have hit this milestone like Ian Koniak, Brandon Fluharty, and Jamal Reimer.

I'll go back to this Werner Erhard concept of "creating your future from the future not your past." A created future means holding on to a vision of successful identity that emanates from who you are being. Change the being, and you get a new doing.

Your future goals need to be 10 to 100X bigger than the ones you set now. And you have to live your life in gratitude as if they're already achieved. Write them down, read them out loud to yourself every day. Own them. Be them. Live life from them. It's a mental (even spiritual) discipline but very achievable. Trust me.

Here's a trick to change your mindset right now. Phrase your goals as though you've already achieved them: "I am grateful to be a 7-figure seller".

These statements (especially spiked with gratitude) imprint into your deeper subconscious and psyche, setting your super bio-computer of a brain on high alert to find every possible pathway to achieve what you want.

Some mindfulness gurus even argue this strategy taps into energies, higher dimensions, and frequencies that science haven't even figured out yet. Goal-setting is broken when you tell yourself you're only going to accomplish something "one day." You'll forever push it out in front of you. You need to start making who you want to be into who you are now. Believe.

You don't attract what you want, you attract what you are.

Needless to say, I'd already read Wallace Wattles 1,000 times and steeped myself in many neo-transcendentalists like Neville Goddard, Ralph Waldo Emerson, and Johann Wolfgang Goethe before meeting Rhonda Byrne who created The Secret. Jack Canfield himself gave me that DVD at a charity auction dinner when I was 26, before it was released.

Rhonda asked me, "What is the longest chapter?" "Gratitude," I immediately answered. She smiled and nodded.

I've found myself drawn to the work of Eckhart Tolle, Byron Katie, and Syd Banks. Consistently, I've learned that the best way to enhance your mindset is to reframe positivity. Drop your negative thoughts as soon as they hit you, and keep and amplify the good ones. Be intentional about how you chronically think. Build a new habituation.

Realize there is only mind, consciousness and thought (3 Principles by Sydney Banks). If you can slow down and pull back from the endless chatter of your thoughts and mind pictures, you can find an inner stillness. You are not your thoughts. "We are living in the feeling of our thinking," per Michael Neill. From this place of peace, your greatest insights appear.

Someone out there is succeeding far more than you: only because they have far greater self-belief. I went down this rabbit hole for a decade and released a hidden paper, my first ever writing called *Musifestation*, on the concept of music-based manifestation.

You can get a free copy of my Musifestation ebook by going to SalesSuperpowers.com/bonus.

Miracles happen when you become aligned or "in tune" with the higher frequencies in the universe (literally, 432 Hz for healing and 528 Hz for miracles). Sometimes the perfect thing you want to happen falls through - but then you realize quite quickly this is the "divine right order of paradise."

It simply wasn't meant to be, and something even better is coming your way. Remember, Pronoia? *The universe is plotting to do you good.*

Right thought yields right action, and turns into manifestation but you can't dwell in the past or your reactive thoughts. You must move from a victim to an owner and creator.

If you'd like to do 7-figure deals, you will need to develop "swagger" and as Jim Mongillo loves to say, "The Swagger breeds." You can never put up a 7-figure deal off a wishy-washy "free pilot" mentality of people-pleasing.

Selling is leading and guiding.

Achieving this level of success requires anchoring the sale high, setting the tone from the first interaction, looking someone in the "whites of their eyes," and shattering that glass of awkwardness by putting forth a number like "1.2MM dollars." Cue Dr. Evil! ;-)

Real executive buyers are accustomed to hearing large amounts of money and when they see that an exec is uncomfortable talking about "the money," they basically get a signal to exploit you.

They see you as "not really a player" rather someone subservient, a pawn that they're going to extract endless free pilots and consulting from.

7-figure closers are honest about what a scaled agreement could look like. They know what's possible, but avoid hyperbole and over-promising.

In the new "post-BANT" reality where "budgets" are gone, executives can create the money. They can pull it from other P&Ls or justify the business case to get the CFO to open up the vault. You should practice saying the full price of your 6-figure enterprise package in front of the mirror as if it's only 5K. Get comfortable with larger figures.

Our childhood experiences shape our comfort level with talking about money. Many of us were conditioned to feel it's the "root of all evil" or that it's impolite/uncivil to "discuss money at the dinner table." This stigma lasts with us as we enter adulthood in enterprise sales and severely limits our comfort level when having honest conversations about the real hard costs of software solutions. If we can even get a seat at the table, we fumble and our palms sweat when discussing money.

But money is just energy. Serve even more. It will come.

One way I encourage you to overcome this hurdle is to look at case studies. When I did this in startups, I found our SaaS customers were averaging a 3 to 10X return and that it was ethical and moral to charge $1MM+ for a solution that predictably returned $3MM to $10MM back to the client within 18 to 36 months.

Return on investment is all relative. If you're selling something with strong product-market fit (PMF) that you believe in - a solution that drives tangible value, you have every right to talk big numbers and defend your pricing. While *The JOLT Effect* by Matt Dixon & Ted McKenna (analyzing 2.5MM sales calles with AI) and much recent research has come out about the power of crafting pilots, I still believe there is something to be said for anchoring high in shaping the tone and tenor of deals.

All the top reps I traveled with did this and as I became a top closer, I did the same. I reflect this in my prospecting methodology to the C-Suite. The way I read Matt Dixon's research, is still anchor high at a production order, but work out an initial pilot with a rock solid commitment to roll into an enterprise license agreement (ELA) upon meeting success criteria milestones. (My friend Jamal Reimer has some great thoughts around closing Mega Deals.)

Matt Dixon nails it paraphrasing, "FOMU - fear of messing up is greater than FOMO - fear of missing out. We must deftly handle indecision by guiding and leading vs. relitigating the status quo." That's why I almost called my method Political Selling, third option: Venn Selling. Let's face it: people want to look good to their boss!

The anatomy of a 7-figure deal therefore starts in your own mind-your limitations with the money conversation, and your willingness to play at this level of spend. I'll never forget Susan St. Ledger, then CRO of the Marketing Cloud, describing the journey with Marc Benioff of the deal sizing at Salesforce over time and the psychology behind it. The value of cloud software kept increasing in ROI and these price points became the natural order of paradise. We are only limited by what we believe in our own mind. Money is energy and simply a gauge of the value of true "service."

CHAPTER 6: GET YOUR JMM PHD

I've spent more than two decades in sales. That's 20+ years of hawking, schlocking, and persuading people to buy everything I could find to sell.

I know how exhausted you've felt - how overwhelmed you may still feel.

Like you, I have put in a lot of hours. Spent entire weeks of sleepless nights on sales strategies, skipping meals, and even ignoring that all-important concept of self-care.

Most of the sales reps I speak to know what it's like to spend hundreds of hours "plugged in." We fall asleep standing up in an airport. We forget which United terminal we're in. I remember falling asleep in a casino in Reno sitting by a railing once.

I tell these stories to highlight that I am not actually an AI. I do not bleed blue beryllium alloy. I'm human just like you.

Like all humans, I know how easy it is to burn out.

So, how do I keep going? The answer goes beyond a greater understanding of TQ and tech stacks.

Technology Quotient (TQ). TQ is our ability to assimilate or adapt to technology changes by developing and employing strategies to successfully include technology in our work and life.

Going *beyond TQ* requires the deft application of two ideas. One is the 80/20 Principle or the Pareto Power Law of Distribution.

The second is the idea of *Selling through Curiosity* as posited by Barry Rhein. He's achieved legendary status delivering sales training in early-stage startups for equity. Some of the organizations he worked with later became behemoths like Salesforce, thanks in no small part to his training.

Let's break down how you can use these concepts to prevent burnout:

I mentioned above, mindset is everything in sales. A positive mental attitude (think UCLA coaching legend John Wooden) is a must, but it's pretty hard to stay positive in a role that is highly commoditized, repetitive, and exhausting. I did it in SaaS for 15 straight years and lived in SB, LA, SF, STL, NYC, SEA, plus Costa Rica!

Pareto in simplicity is this:

Review your day. Admit that 80% is waste. Hone in on the 20% where 80% of your effectiveness comes from. Handoff the other (wasteful) 80% to your AI-assistant team, a VA, or just cut it out. Now go 10X even 100X on the 20% that actually yields results…

If you apply this literally, you'll get insane outcomes. Less is more, more with less. Wait, stop the presses? More with less? Yes, it's Physics and Asymmetry. If you have 80% garbage output, turn that off, and do a lot more of the 20% gold input. Suddenly, all the remaining systems evolve.

It works for marathon training, diets, entrepreneurship, romance – all human endeavors. It's just math!

Applying TQ IRL:

So, how can you boost your technology quotient? Coaching platforms like our own Hard Skill Exchange, which can be found at the website hardskill.exchange, are ideal for 1:1 situational simulations that allow for safe competency transfer. Alternatively, you could explore courses from Josh Braun and Justin Welsh, and look into private sales training and mastermind groups with yours truly to get certified on the JMM, even try your hand at tech stack consulting (a newly emerging field) kicked off by *Tech-Powered Sales*. YOU need to make a decision to become one with your technology exoskeleton and AI overlords.

There are a bunch of Trailheads on Salesforce that are affordable and give you a badge *you can actually use* to advance in your career. You can join private Slack Channel micro-communities to uplevel like HYPCCCYCL (the one I co-founded with Julia Nimchinski), Pavilion, Wizard of Ops, and SalesStack.io.

I even created a *Fight Club* model as a mastermind group that floats on WhatsApp & Discord globally with the world's most elite outbound practitioners. Conducting all my business on WhatsApp is a superpower. I encourage you to leverage "real-time" mediums yourself and experience the thrill of "zero-time selling," client creation and fulfillment. (Hat tip Andy Paul)

As I aspire to become the Tony Stark of prospecting with sales tech stacks, (in a similar way that Aaron Ross became the Henry Ford for the new sales supply chain as defined in *Predictable Revenue - 2011*), it's only natural I'd assemble a ragtag band of beautiful misfits going rogue called "Salesborgs" to fully disrupt revenue operations (RevOps) as we know it. (Take the RevTQ test at Salesborgs.ai to see how your TQ stacks up against the industry.)

My tribe is obsessed with hacking each other's tech stacks on Zoom calls, breaking down cold emails, and endlessly debating "RevOps." Modern tech stacks (or Frankenstacks, as I sarcastically call them) are a Rube Goldberg machine of complexity, crying out to be MacGyvered by elite JMM practitioners and ever simplified by AI advancements. Check out the free academies from Outreach, SalesLoft, Apollo.io, and Groove, and educate yourself.

Decide to upskill with a new passion for curiosity.

If you only learn one thing from my writings it's this: Be more curious! That's it. That is a million-dollar piece of advice.

Our prospects are fascinating people. You're just not listening. At least I wasn't, and for a decade that was the key piece holding me back in sales.

Peel the onion, and get to know your potential customers. Find out what they had for breakfast last week, genuinely ask about their weekend, their work history, their hobbies, motivations, and their passions. Make sure you know their organization so well, they start to see you as a colleague, rather than a vendor.

Remember the 10Ks and 10Qs are still skin deep. You need to navigate their culture, their politics, their fears, and come up with a SWOT Analysis hanging in the balance. How do you do this? By being more curious! The more curiosity you cultivate, the harder it is to burn out.

Every day is fascinating. Have you seen the French film Amélie? All Audrey Tautou does is try to be the most epic do-gooder of all time, by helping everyone around her behind the scenes.

So, take the same approach. Make it all about your customer, their success, enhancement, and growth. A vaunted trusted advisor status has become the holy grail of selling. If we can only become a trusted advisor, 7-figure enterprise deals unlock seamlessly. But how to do it has eluded most of us… I've found Charles H. Green's superb books on *trust-based selling* are a great start on how to develop timeless trustworthiness and business acumen. Read the

Go-Giver by Bob Burg – single biggest life transformation: a life of service as sales. Pay it forward!

Bonus points: Your attitude determines your altitude. Develop an indestructible growth mindset at all times.

You miss 100% of the shots you don't take, per Gretzky - ranked by Sports Illustrated as the most dominant athlete of all time. There's no way you're going to make millions being super negative unless maybe you're an undertaker. ;-) Positive psychology creates a "flow state." Positive energy makes people like you.

Think Dale Carnegie. Without even broaching the quantum physics implications of a good attitude, what I can say is a Growth Mindset á la Carol Dweck in her hit book *Mindset* is an X factor in business success.

We can't fully control what happens in the world around us. However, we can control how we respond to those events.

E + R = O is an equation my mentor Jack Canfield taught me. Only the R is within our domain, truly. How we choose to Respond.

We start with the event: A forest catches fire (E). We (R) respond: stay positive and deploy super scoopers to drop water, and a new Outcome (O) emerges: doused, a new forest grows from the ashes.

Business blows up (E), response (stay optimistic), a new, unexpected MORE lucrative partnership (O), and thereby better new business emerges.

The new forest and better business could never form without some creative destruction. This doesn't mean you fly blind in life. It means that a concerted, positive, can-do attitude where you believe you can grow, change, and get better is everything.

Approach every day, company, technology, and life situation with a Beginner's Mind. The wisest coaches, managers, technologists approach life this way. The way of the Samurai in the words of Miyamoto Mushashi, "Today is victory over yourself of yesterday; tomorrow is your victory over lesser men."

To master your craft and prevent burn out, follow these simple tips. You'll be an unstoppable BEAST. You don't need a cyborg, machine, or AI to thrive. All you need is self-awareness and self-actualization driving you from a mission-focused place.

One last point: which is the greatest trade secret of all. The Masters in any field know it. Driving revenue is powerful but what's even more powerful? Driving a mission forward in the world and as a result, kicking off revenue. If you have a mission beyond simply money, you can work without ceasing, and it feels like play. Even a hard slog. Maybe you're reading this just waking up from a plate of food your head fell into or napping in some airport. Don't lose heart. It only gets better! From acorns, oaks... !

If you are ever blue or depressed, reach out to someone and serve them. Trust me, it makes a difference.

GPT Lab: Get Curious!
_____

Although GPT doesn't know curiosity, it can pattern match on it.

Here's a few ideas on prompts that build curiosity:

1. List five 'what if' questions about different aspects of life or the universe that make you wonder about the possibilities.

2. Choose an ordinary object or phenomenon and brainstorm at least three unusual uses or explanations for it, pushing the limits of your creativity.

3. Pick a topic you know little about and generate three questions that, if answered, would deepen your understanding or spark further exploration.

Interview Mastery

At this point, you might be wondering how to get to the next stage in your career, or start a new sales venture from scratch.

Unlocking amazing opportunities in the sales landscape requires the use of many of the techniques in this book, from adjusting your mindset, to rethinking how you communicate with others.

I once read a book called *60 seconds and You're Hired* by Robin Ryan and quickly realized the error of my ways with interviewing. Now I suggest it to all my clients. All that matters is focusing on *why* they are interviewing you. What is the outcome they are looking to achieve?

I used to look up at the ceiling when I got asked a tough question. I was unwilling to really pause, just sit there and let the time span out and hang. If they ask you a Barbara Walters question, you're better off just answering it bluntly, rather than rambling.

Never, ever share your W-2 (income history). Fortunately, in most geographies now, you're legally protected from being coerced to do so.

You actually don't need to give your income history in interviews-did you realize that? In fact, doing so could be detrimental. Why generate one offer when you could get multiple offer letters at once and create a bidding war?

In the words of Lee Bartlett, "You screen your employer, not the other way around." I'm a firm believer in this. You need a great boss, not a toxic energy vampire.

"Your method works for getting recruited," wrote my client in Dubai. "I built out an account-based sales development (ABSD) Tracker to fill my bench with job opportunities. I've used all the JMM principles for the interview cycle itself. Using your methods (triples + RRM + VM drops) I booked myself 5 tech sales interviews this week."

One of my favorite tactics is to blitz the hiring manager with cold calls and then unleash my trusted network one degree away from them, to send letters of recommendation by email and LinkedIn pre-emptively.

Then I deploy every connection in common that may know them and me, asking them to put in a good word. When they see that level of political savvy and networked intelligence demonstrated, you show (not tell) them a very compelling reason to hire you.

When I first started interviewing, I would get defensive and combat the interviewer whenever they poked holes in my resume. I remember getting turned down for an inside sales role at Oracle with a tribunal of 9 people because I was so defensive about "my lack of continuing education." "Why wouldn't you pursue higher ed?" they asked. That really offended me and I just got increasingly belligerent the more they questioned my CV.

So, how did I overcome this? Simply put, I built my bench. I've literally applied to thousands of jobs. I mean that - *thousands*. I remember the number haunting me every time I logged into my LinkedIn jobs section.

Some of the more famous companies I ended up working with initially rejected me automatically. Their system for applicant tracking immediately noticed my lack of a college degree, and purged me from the candidate list. But this didn't stop me - and it shouldn't stop you either. The chances are, if you're not a little overwhelmed by the number of roles you're applying for, you're probably not applying enough.

Another step in my strategy, I recommend to others, is to have your resume professionally rewritten by a resume writer. There are ways that a CV needs to look and read that graduates from Stanford, Harvard, and Wharton know. These experts can infuse your resume with signals that act like a "secret handshake" to hiring managers.

Crucially, making a great impression with your resume doesn't mean crafting a fake version of yourself - no matter how tempting it seems. I even had some recruiters advise me to put "some college" on my resume because I'd attended some night school uni extension programs for graphic design back in the day.

Honesty will always take you further than a lie. As soon as you're asked to expand on that "college education" you never really got, you risk permanently damaging your reputation in the eyes of your prospective employer.

Additionally, remember that interviews are always going to have their challenging components, no matter how prepared you feel you are. When you get asked a tough question in an interview, just own it, talk less than 60 seconds, and move on. Or ask a thoughtful question in return.

Over time I began to ace all my job interviews using these methods. I stopped thinking about "me" and what I needed from a role, and started focusing on how my unique experiences could help other companies reach their goals.

Just like prospects, business leaders and hiring managers want to hear what's "in it for them." They want you to tell them you're going to lead their company in outbound dials every day, and become the best cold caller they've ever seen.

They want to hear you explain how every job experience you had has helped you to become the ultimate addition to their team. After you make it all about them, you start to rack up unlimited job offers. By the age of 40, I was receiving 6 offers at once, and it's part of what prompted me to branch out on my own as an independent consultant.

Case study: When I moved to Silicon Valley at 31, I swallowed my pride. I must have applied to something in the region of 5,000 jobs. I was rejected repeatedly by Salesforce and LinkedIn - companies I later worked for. Kudos to forward-thinking CEOs who lifted the college degree requirement and are now hiring on merit. Sales ability is the great equalizer. If you become phenomenal at pipeline generation by learning the mindsets, skill sets and tactics laid out in this book, you will forever be in demand.

From a mindset perspective in the interview - remember: you are interviewing them. But when they throw out, "What questions do you have for me?" don't think it isn't a trap! Always flip it back to asking about additional ways to drive value for them. So when they ask this question try a response like this?

1. What other ways have salespeople been effective on your team?
2. Which of your channels is performing highest?
3. How is marketing supporting the sales team?

I encourage you to sit down with the CEO, CMO, and even CRO, if you are going after a VP of Sales position. Go out to lunch with all of them. I've been in multiple interview cycles with over 9 interviews. The more connections you make, the harder it is to simply "reject" you. Follow up after every interview with a few bullets to summarize what you learned, how you think you can execute in the future, and express gratitude for their time.

My last point is you should always create a bidding war with no less than 3 offers. Why? To up your base salary. You'll need to make a judgment call if you disclose who the offers are from or keep them anonymous. Once you have one offer on the table, you can alert the two others and they'll usually play ball.

Always counter once; you will typically get offered a 10-15% higher base. Keep in mind, if you counter too many times they may punish you for this or close the door on the opportunity, so be cautious.

In closing, whenever you update your resume, go back to your professional resume writer for help. They know the "Harvard Yard" syntax and "skull & bones" secret handshake for how stuff needs to be written to appeal to recruiters. While I'm partially tongue-in-cheek here, sadly, I can't change this system for now. I can just teach you how to optimize it if like me, you have a nontraditional background and are breaking into software sales.

Analogies aside, even without a degree, once I had my CV face-lifted for a few hundred bucks, it opened up bidding wars and opportunities like getting hired by Sean Parker. Swallow your pride and hire a pro.

Getting promoted In Under 6 months

So now you're hired - what's next?

Earning a promotion.

How many reps do you know that, despite being the best at what they do, never get promoted, or suddenly hit an income ceiling?

Have you ever wondered why that happens? Next in line to the throne often follows the Peter Principle. You'll only get promoted to the highest level of incompetence in the organization. So if your manager is an ignoramus, good luck.

We talked about politics and optics. Good news travels fast, so you should share it immediately. If you're on a sales team, you should still be close with your CRO, CEO and Co-Founders. Make friends in the C-Suite genuinely.

Be the source of "new revenue." Constantly update Slack and bang the gong with new opportunities. Be a river to your people. When you do this, upper management thinks: "Hey, let's give them their own team and make 5 more 'mini-mes.'"

If you're the person booking meetings, you're always going to work.

I once locked myself in a cubicle and did 50 triples per day for 90 days. When I came up for air, I led the world in a new pipeline using the methods that became *COMBO Prospecting*, and I was given the entire global SDR division in 8 countries of an 80MM run rate business. Can you put your head down today and commit to 1-2 hours? The compound effect of this over a quarter is astounding. (Remember the 900 Challenge)

> *"When you set yourself on fire, people love to come and see you burn." – John Wesley*

Managing "optics" is a greater determinant of internal promotion than your sales skill. It's the whole "if a bear sh$#s in the woods, who hears it?" If you're so efficient in your role that you become basically invisible, what's the incentive for management to promote you? What's going to force them to take notice?

The easiest way to boost your chances of promotion, is to show your leaders how more responsibility and opportunity for you will benefit them. Take work off your direct manager's plate. Present them with easy ways to streamline their day.

Take on RevOps elements like list building, vetting new software, automating procedures, recruiting, and start helping uplevel the performance of others on your team. By doing this I was often given "dotted line" responsibility over the entire global SDR team within weeks of showing up in a company as a senior AE, Director or RVP.

I went beyond my job description, and demonstrated the value of positioning me in a higher role.

There is a hidden meritocracy in startup companies and often crazy busy CROs will just hand you a cool project or initiative if you show leadership. Oftentimes it sticks. The faster you can help your sales leaders hit their targets, the more integral you will become to "the plan" even if you can't always see that. They'll rewrite you into it!

One secret I used for advancement was demonstrating a willingness to always be a "player-coach." I was never once a professional paper pushing, spreadsheet jockey manager who solely updated the forecast and did 1:1s with my people. I'm not discounting how important that stuff is for the smooth functioning of a revenue org but I was also carrying my own number and an overlay percentage.

You can rapidly advance in software companies if you are willing to carry a quota, coach reps, and run teams direct or dotted line. I realize this shredded my time and ultimately meant I was doing over 70-hour weeks - but when, like me, you're climbing the ladder from nowhere with no degree, the extra work pays off. How bad do you want it in this pursuit of happiness? (Great and relevant film!)

It doesn't just show your leaders that you're a true "go-getter." It also means you have access to more opportunities. The more responsibility you take on, the more you "learn by doing." Your skills and values evolve.

Don't underestimate the importance of building the right internal relationships too.

Once a GM made me an RVP and I left a very prestigious role to accept the title upgrade. Unfortunately, that GM was then fired within weeks of me entering the position. Losing my internal champion made it nearly impossible for me to maintain political capital, thrive in the role, or achieve my sales goals.

That's why top reps often follow managers across multiple companies. You need an internal C-Suite executive that can go to bat for your compensation, pay plan, SPIFFs, and push hard on the CFO to get your bonuses paid out. The best sales jobs pay on signings (not bookings, when the firm is paid) so there's steady cash coming in.

Be willing to take a clawback for this setup because, again, the "time value" of money is very real. Cash in hand is worth way more to you than endlessly waiting around for the company to be paid on net-90 quarterly terms, so you can get your sliver of commission.

Any managers or CXOs reading this: pay your people on signings, and you will attract the top reps in the industry. Reps like immediate cash. Period.

Dominating Side hustles

40% of reps side hustle - and why shouldn't they?

What if you could pull down an extra 5-20K/mo consulting, advising, and teaching your unique skills, or just generating sales and leads for other ventures, *non-competitively*? With a side hustle, you can.

Back in my day, if you even contributed to a sales book in your spare time it was considered "moonlighting." That's why my name isn't mentioned in *COMBO Prospecting* (I'm the anonymous 'cyborg' case study). As long as you're not doing something competitive to the mothership, it probably won't cause problems. But some big corps, even consider how you sell, *their* I.P – not yours.

Conversely, your open-minded, servant-leader/direct manager may even give you carte blanche as long as it doesn't eat into productivity and selling time in the "golden hours" of your 9 to 5.

My first advice when it comes to side hustling, is to find the distinction between "gifts" and "talents." Gifts come so easy to you, they're like breathing, and so we often overlook them. Talents are the things we could be good at. Because they're harder to develop we grind away on them missing our inherent gifts. We mistakenly believe cultivating our talents will eventually lead to mastery.

My counterintuitive advice is: once you find your gift, push that one so extreme it becomes hard. Then, you can become truly *great*. So what's your side hustle? (Choose something that's non-competitive to your employer).

Options:

Coaching reps: check out a new platform invented by Julia Nimchinski that I co-founded just launched out of stealth: Hardskill.
Exchange (apply now to become coach!)

Ghostwriting or DFY (done-for-you) content and social media
marketing (SMM): How many execs do you know who can't write
like you or admire your content? Time-poor, maybe they need
help managing their social media presence or building their personal brand with bespoke content?

Recruiting: so many sales leaders are already great at this. You're
just monetizing your network and matchmaking - you can earn
20% of placements or offer to take a lower percentage and un-
dercut the majors.

Appointment setting: Take on 1-2 clients on the side and just get
them quality meetings in an hour or two a day call blitz.

Building out email sequences/cadences: You'd be surprised – you
can get paid thousands for these (especially if they produce results), as even many team leads can't get out of the white space.
ChatGPT is disrupting this one at the speed of light, but you can
learn to harness the AI and be the last mile editor so it achieves
JMM levels.

It's a myth that you can only have one income. Again, as Marylou
Tyler shares, "You are a razor and each income stream is another
blade." At this writing, I have 12 income streams and I'll probably
hit 15.

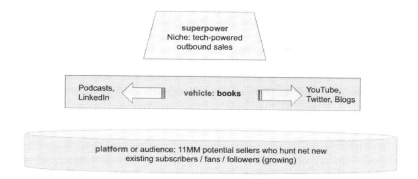

Your platform, vehicle, and superpower

You should write a book and do public speaking. (I might know a publisher!) These moves establish credibility and authority and give you a vehicle or Michael Hyatt *Platform* to springboard all your entrepreneurial endeavors.

Ask yourself: what are all the ways you can monetize your gifts in your sleep? If you use the 80/20 rule to get your day job down to just a few hours per day, it creates time for you to open up additional income streams.

Since the tax code in the US will probably never change, realize the following: You can work both 1099 and W-2 as long as you pay taxes on every last penny to Uncle Sam. Secondarily, getting healthcare on the private exchange, although much more costly than while working for an employer, is not crippling.

Your ability to do consulting and take on many clients concurrently makes it lucrative enough to forget about this extra expense. If you go solo, you can also get an LLC, S or C Corp, and write off a lot more of your expenses; travel (for clients!), mileage, office space (1/3rd of your home) etc. Caveat: Consult a qualified tax professional, CPA or M&A attorney to assess your options here.

One thing new consultants and coaches struggle with is insecurity. They falsely believe they're not "worthy enough" to succeed and struggle with impostor syndrome. You gain confidence via market validation and as you start creating results for clients. One of the best ways to rapidly launch a side hustle is to coach/consult some friends for free in return for glowing testimonials.

Your confidence will jump reading your testimonial file and you can socialize them to other 1st circle connections, charging a nominal fee to gain a healthy book of business out of the starting gate.

Grab those consulting hours, and then take those testimonials to your 2nd degree circle. This will pack your calendar with coaching and consulting, get you that initial pool of screaming fans of your service, and build your self esteem like crazy. The more you coach/consult, the better you'll get at it and the higher the fees you can charge.

Cal Newport's gem of a book, *So Good They Can't Ignore You*, changed my thinking here. You can chase your passion, change lives, and make a phenomenal living. That's why I never charge less than my best attorney – and you shouldn't either!

But take baby steps getting up that ladder.

My law of fees: If you charge too much, you'll feel guilty you're not providing enough value. If you charge too little, you'll feel exploited. So find that Goldilocks Zone in the middle, and never work by the hour.

Read consulting mastery books by the luminous Alan Weiss and David C. Baker to master how to leverage your expertise, build practical proposals, and validate yourself in the market.

GPT Lab: Hustle Builder

Help GPT help you build a side hustle by using this prompt:

You are a career counselor and I'm looking to start a side business. Can you provide guidance on the following topics, asking me any necessary questions to answer these topics.

Start with 3 brief questions, and when you ask a single question stop until I respond with [star emoji]

After the initial 3 questions, give me responses, and then further iterate based on my answers to subsequent questions:

- Defining my goals for the business
- Identifying my skills, interests, and experiences
- Determining my target audience
- Developing products or services to offer
- Creating a business model
- Planning the necessary resources to start and operate the business
- Outlining a marketing plan
- Complying with legal and regulatory requirements

I'd appreciate any advice or insights you can offer."

Scaling Outbound

"After reading Tech-Powered Sales, an idea was born to set up a dedicated sales operations team and invest heavily in tech and data.

This decision allowed us to specialize resources and I believed it played a big part in us having a positive retention rate throughout the year (we are seeing more client expansion than churn).

163

We worked with Justin to set up a framework that can be replicated across all clients and all industries. We implemented the framework first on our internal SDR team.

The results are pretty impressive when it comes to metrics. We are seeing a significant increase in open rates, reply rates, connection rates, and meeting conversion rates. The most impressive thing however is that his method is unleashing SDR creativity. Reps are having fun and are no longer intimidated by prospects. And this is translating into results.

One SDR was so bored in the role that he was considering if this is the right job for him. Now he is becoming one of the top-performing SDRs that we ever had. Another SDR was struggling with setting meetings - she set 4 in a day and never looked back.

Other SDRs are asking their managers: when is the JMM going to be implemented on their accounts? If you ever ran an SDR team - you will know that very few people are excited to do the work.

If you are in the process of setting up a high-performing sales development operation, his content and coaching are a must-have. – Darko Davkovski, COO, Growth Era

My big idea is front-burner / back-burner: you take 20 percent of your targets, the truly VIP group, and hyper-personalize your approach to them with manual COMBO motions. The other 80% you can fully automate leveraging "Relevance at Scale."

Emails simply work like ad units, and should be hyper-short to reflect our prospects' attention span. This works like ad "segmentation & targeting"- you get ±18 words from the preview text to the subject line. When you serve ads, you typically pick a geography and demographic, so be specific.

I call this the minimum viable grouping. Imagine you have 1,000 prospects. Then challenge yourself to break it down into the smallest numbers of sequences based on commonalities between them.

While I've built persona matrices frequently, the better approach to sequencing is Occam's Razor. Figure out the least amount of sequences you need across verticals and titles within your ideal customer profile (ICP). Example: VPs of Marketing in FinTech, Strategic Decision Makers in E-Commerce and Agencies. Then write one master sequence that will resonate with that group. At minimum, I'd want to build a strategic sequence and technical sequence, for each project.

"Right now, a sales team has three options to scale outbound. Option one is continue hiring BDRs. Bad option. Option two: extremely high volume with templatized outreach. Not targeted, not personalized – burns your domain reputation. The third option is Clay. com, an outbound engine to scale your outbound motion without scaling head count.

Now you can replace an entire BDR team, integrate 50+ data providers with AI included out-of-the-box. Every message is personalized (you save time and money while the meeting-booked-rate goes up). You can even scale with RevOps alone. In fact one client, cut 50% of their sales team, and revenue went up using Clay. Humans don't go away, they get to do higher leveraged things that can't be automated. " – Varun Anand, Head of Operations

LEADING AI VENDORS & MINDS TO KEEP ON YOUR RADAR:

The French visionary to watch in this space is Maxence de Ville-pion from CARGO that came out of Y Combinator S23. Cargo helps revenue teams unify their company data to easily segment, score and route qualified leads to sales reps to let them focus on selling.

Centralize your data story with tools like Syncari, a company leading the way to automated data orchestration layers.

Erol Toker at Truly is doing wild things with "robots" to fully automate SDR workflows, challenging traditional CRM.

My protegé Eric Nowoslawski is a shining star of the AI-based personalization movement; don't miss his YouTube channel for hands-on tactics to scale JMM™ with tools like Clay that integrate 50+ sources for hyper-personalization (HYPER-P).

And let's not forget CIENCE 2.0's AI-voice calls and Rightbound, both achieving the autonomous top funnel reality that crosses the Uncanny Valley as predicted back in 2020 in my bestseller with Tony J. Hughes, *Tech-Powered Sales*, you can find it at TechPoweredSalesBook.com.

Greg Meyer & Soham Sarkar would argue that every step of the sales supply chain can be influenced, augmented or replaced by OpenAI's GPT.

The two big forces to scale outbound are *subspecialization* and *consolidation*, big shout out to John Girard (former CEO of Cience) for helping to clarify my thinking here. You must *moneyball* the best traits out of your people. Social sellers focus on LinkedIn. Hardcore callers stay on the phones – invest in a parallel-assisted dialer (PAD). Make one analytical rep a data analyst to create the best lists and enrich them. Build a sophisticated virtual assistant (VA) operation with Aditya Prakash.

Drop one head count to increase your investment on tech stack per rep. All these top-of-funnel (TOFU) roles will be replaceable with machine learning algorithms and neural nets by 2025 and go fully autonomous well before 2035. *Predictable Revenue* by Aaron Ross and *The Machine* by Justin Roff-Marsh are good foundations to disrupt the prevailing SDR-AE "Industrial Complex."

If you're running a sales team now, make a solid investment in the following areas:

1. Top reps for top funnel (not green – or provide phenomenal onboarding)
2. Strategic full-cycle sales training for openers too!
3. Best-of-breed tech stacks up to $5,000/mo/rep (mind blown yet?! - think about the cost to equip Navy Seals)
4. Training on the tech stack. I might know a guy! ;-)

My issue with books like *The Machine* that evangelize changing up the roles, functions, and processes in the sales org is they seldom take into account the exponential growth curves of generative/cognitive AI innovation which will quickly automate out 100% of the top funnel and supplant many other aspects of GTM. Not to mention when we reach the Singularity. Ironically, *The Machine* does not include the greatest self-learning machine of all: AI. That said - it's a brilliant read.

Yes, we can *Moneyball* our bench of talent with specialization to optimize how we go to market like pro baseball. But with AI, opening motions will evaporate, and we'll return very rapidly to 'full cycle' inside sales down-funnel, so the training and tech stack enablement must change to keep pace. Our entire GTM strategy must be rethought based on where humans are even needed in the loop, and the implications are threefold:

1. Humans must learn to prompt AIs (becoming GPT Whisperers)

2. We must all become adept at training the machines via RLHF "reinforced learning from human feedback" (very soon machines will simply train themselves)
3. Ironically, with higher conversation rates, humans will need to learn how to sell human-to-human (H2H) again

The outbound reps of the future will need high technology quotient (TQ) or to upskill it to compete. TQ, as distinct from IQ and EQ, is defined as the ability for human and machine to fuse in "tech-powered" selling. Renaissance reps will need to focus on this new discipline along with cultivating a data science understanding. So you're not technical? I've got bad news for you. Your success in the future will also hinge greatly on mastery of low to no-code software engineering techniques. But don't worry, it's going to look a lot more like *Minority Report* or Jarvis vs. a hackathon than we think. Helpful bots will always be one blink away like in the film *Her*.

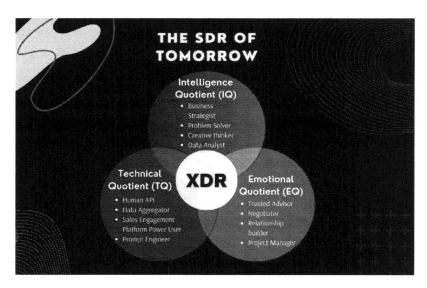

Diagram by Charles Needham

"We will increasingly see the top human salespeople being asked to work with deep learning engineers to more or less teach AI algorithms how to understand human emotions, build relationships with customers, and fulfill the simplest parts of the sales process." – Ben Daters

Creating the best possible sales team culture is about MT&R, as Ichak Adizes evangelizes: "mutual trust and respect." Your virtual door must remain open: no gossiping or talking behind others' backs. Maintain open, transparent, authentic communication at all times and empathy. Everyone is fighting a hidden emotional battle you can't see. Morale is driven by productivity and getting results. Action bias is contagious. Teamwork is good for mental health.

Leaders of the future must create an environment where taking 10X massive action is the rule, not the exception. This takes tremendous self-belief. A culture where no one is afraid to "move fast, and break things" only works when your customer is placed at the center. (Hat tip Julia Nimchinski.) Make intelligent mistakes and fail forward. As Reid Hoffman says most poetically about startups, "you throw yourself off a cliff and build an airplane on the way down." ;-)

I was always the rep that prospected the most even during "ramp up." It's always day one, and it's better to talk to a potential customer now than waste three months of productivity on acquiring "product knowledge." You ultimately need that too. Like Ian Koniak says, "Obsess over RGAs- daily revenue generating activities," and you will leave everyone in the dust. Play full out as a leader. Be the lead cyclist in the Peloton and your team can draft off of you.

"Culture eats strategy for breakfast." – Peter Drucker

I landed a lucrative SaaS gig once when I shared this quote with a CEO. Leaders build leaders. The leader is the culture. As a leader, do you make cold calls? I *still* do.

Explosive pipeline reduces infighting as internecine warfare breaks out whenever revenue is chronically down.

Don't *super-close* your reps' deals by going around them, but show your vulnerability and humanity by hopping on zooms and cold calling with them, providing candid coaching feedback. Share your worst rejection messages. Level the playing field; we are all in this together, running this rejection-dense gauntlet we call outbound sales.

Never fire anyone on your team - stiffen discipline and they'll naturally quit if they're not meant to work with you. Simply define and inspect high performance activity KPIs. With one client, I'm already implementing the 55 min LinkedIn workout from this book to help turn around a failing rep and spike results across the board. What's the portfolio of omnichannel daily prospecting touches you're going to measure? Build an accountability scorecard or dashboard and make sure everyone can view it 24/7.

As Peter Drucker stated so eloquently, "only what gets measured, gets managed." If you start paying attention to the DOING, the reps who were phoning it in (or *not* phoning!), will leave of their own accord.

Signal-based Prospecting: A Blueprint to Scale Relevance

Sales teams have a simple but often incorrect mental model for prospecting.

They assume they can find a list of contacts from a data provider, add them to a sequencer, and a new pipeline will automatically follow.

Unfortunately, there are a number of issues here. SDRs are 71% less effective at connecting with decision-makers than they were 10 years ago. They're making 55% more attempts per contact (calls, emails, LinkedIn touches, etc.) but they're getting 55% less conversions: connected calls, email replies, etc.

(See the Bridge Group's *SDR Metrics Report* for updated stats on this.)

We're going to cover the 9 reasons why SDRs are becoming less effective, a 4-step framework for outbound that's relevant at scale, and specific plays your team can make to implement this today.

In the last 10 years, the pace of business has dramatically increased due to the smartphone. You are always reachable by smartphone by multiple channels: Linkedin, email, cell phone, Slack, Whatsapp, and so on.

Part of the reason the JMM method works in the first place is it's optimized for mobile... but the increase in volume from mass adoption of sales sequencers is taking its toll.

(Thanks Scott Martinis)

9 Reasons Outbound is getting harder

REASON 1: MOBILE INFORMATION OVERLOAD

In the mobile-first attention economy, sales reps aren't just competing against other sales reps, they're competing with texts from the buyer's spouse/partner, social media notifications, news articles, personal emails notifications, fitness app notifications, even *Candy Crush*.

Reason 2: Outbound Volume Tech

Sequencing technology has hit the mainstream, and inbox rotation and parallel dialing tech is close behind. Sales teams are massively increasing volume with tech instead of headcount.

Reason 3: Missing/Bad Contact Data

Big name providers sometimes have email lists with 30%+ bounce rates, and 50% mobile/direct dial coverage if that. That means 30-50% of your market might not be reachable in a scalable way, and the ones that are reachable are getting bombarded with outbound messaging.

Reason 4: Emails are going to spam

Google and Microsoft are responding to the growth in email volume by tightening spam filters, ultimately getting CEO emails sent to spam. There's an urban legend that one startup needed to get Sequoia to introduce them to the CTO of Microsoft... so their domain could be whitelisted after the sales team blew it up.

Reason 5: Calls are going to spam

Cell phones are now spam-filtering inbound calls, and many sales dialers aren't paying attention to their spam listings. If you aren't checking, your sales team's calls to cell phones could be falling into the void.

Reason 6: Buyers have individual channel preferences

Buyers are solving the noise of smartphones by picking channels they are most comfortable with. Frequent Linkedin posters accept connection requests and reply to DMs faster and more consistently. People brave enough to pick up unknown phone calls do so consistently. A few disciplined buyers hit inbox zero every day.

The flipside of that is some of your prospects will never pick up the phone, or answer a Linkedin DM, or reply to emails. And trying to MAKE those prospects respond will result in them marking your calls, emails, and connection requests as spam.

REASON 7: INDUSTRIES ARE 30%+ WRONG IN DATA PROVIDERS

Look at Bumble and Salesforce on Linkedin. One is a dating app, the other is a B2B software company, both categorized as "software" companies. Data providers scraped Linkedin, patted themselves on the back, and let sellers sort out the inaccurate lists.

Spoiler: they usually don't. Imagine the frustration of 100+ contact attempts a day from people that don't even understand your business model.

REASON 8: DIFFERENT BUYER SOLUTION PREFERENCES

You aren't selling to a person, you're selling to a company culture.

Imagine two 200 employee SaaS companies. One is a diehard inbound team filled with titles like "demand gen," "community," "content," and so on. The other is mostly outbound with SDRs, AEs, and a couple generic "marketing" titles that basically run trade shows and sales collateral.

Imagine emailing "marketers" within each of those teams. To win, you need to identify *buyer belief systems* at scale.

REASON 9: SELLERS TALK ABOUT THEIR PRODUCT, NOT THE PROSPECT'S TOP PROBLEMS

Neurologically, scarcity and desperation shut down empathy. When sellers are desperate to hit quota and don't have a system, they just talk about their product.

Outbound always works if you talk about one of your buyer's top problems (Jason Lemkin), but if your team doesn't have a systematic way to build empathy like the JMM method or the SIRI method to follow, failure is likely.

The SIRI Framework

The problem with lots of personalization is that it won't last once buyers are educated to realize it's fake. Personalization that works forever, works when it's relevant to the prospect.

The SIRI framework is a systematic way for your team to craft relevant messaging.

SIRI: SIGNAL, INFERENCE, RESULT, INVITE

Signal: Identify a clear, unambiguous signal about your prospect that indicates they have a problem you can solve. "Free trial" on their website, 5-10 sales reps, new CMO, RevOps title.

Signals allow you to 10x volume while maintaining relevance

Inference: Infer a problem or need based on the signal you observed. E.g. They need to rapidly scale the sales team because of Series A, trouble converting trials into paid customers, they need more detailed reporting because they have a RevOps title.

Inference shows you understand your prospect which gets them to connect with you.

Result: What result can you give to the buyer that is relevant to the problem you think they have? Keep this short and punchy, mention a metric or accomplishment that could get them promoted or hired at a higher paying job.

Results are what earns your prospect's attention

<u>Invite:</u> Invite them to a specific next step. Send some content, learn more, book a call, discuss, share if the result is relevant or if they have the problem you think they have.

A clear invitation increases the chance of response by reducing confusion and risk for the prospect.

Table Stakes Plays

So how can you use the SIRI framework to actually scale outbound? Here are 6 steps to start today.

Step 1: Make sure all outbound systems you are using are correctly set up. Domain setup including SPF, DKIM, DMARC at the time of writing, this might change in the future.

Step 2: Check if your communication channels are going to spam. Call a personal cell with your phone number, email your personal email or use a testing service. DM a friend on Linkedin. Make sure your outbound actually gets through

Step 3: Filter for clean data. Don't use guessed emails or phones in your data provider; have at minimum a level of automated verification.

Step 4: Add a few more filters to your outbound. Department headcount, some keywords, maybe headcount growth. Filter out the prospects you wouldn't want to talk to up front.

Step 5: Spot check your messaging against SIRI. Are you talking about the prospect's biggest problem? Could you help them get promoted based on the message you sent. If you got this message, would it go at the top of your to-do list? Rewrite if not.

Step 6: Personalize the first touch. If you don't have the technical sophistication to personalize at scale, spend 3 minutes per prospect to personalize. (*If you don't have time, per JMM, do 30 sec-*

onds.) This doesn't just improve replies, it makes it less likely that your messaging will go to spam.

Intermediate Plays

Contact & channel validation

Have VAs or AI check your contact data to make sure it's valid, and if prospects are responsive on that channel. This can more than triple your connection and response rates.

Build a "signal" playbook
Write out the best signals for your solution. A great way to frame this: What would the perfect prospect's Linkedin profile, team, website, etc. look like?
Answer this question, then start talking about the potential business problems you can infer from those signals.
Build signal-based lists
Map these signals into your data providers or find VAs or custom tech to scrape them for you. If your signals are mapped into your tools, relevance becomes much easier to scale.

Build sequences targeted to each signal
Craft specific sequences aimed at each signal. These can be evergreen: every company that gets a new CMO can be added to this list. Since the signal is predictable, the pain and desired result can be too.

AI personalization
At the time of this writing, there are numerous vendors for AI personalization. They will work if the personalization is actually relevant to the prospect, or if the buyer isn't aware it's personalized at scale. Test it through the lens of relevance.

Email Volume Tech

If you have signals built out, then scaling volume makes sense. At the time of writing, email warming, secondary domains, and inbox rotation are the most common way to do that. Custom IPs, custom mail servers, and subdomains with warming are another.

If you're a small business and don't worry much about compliance, secondary domains are a useful way to scale with the right software.

This isn't for the faint of heart as you will need to do a lot of work to connect with your CRM. Many of these tools aren't well integrated right now.

As they're adopted at scale, Google and Microsoft may crack down as well.

Call Volume Tech
Assuming a clean contact list and a good cold call, power or parallel dialers are an amazing addition to your sales team. Currently you can hit 10+ conversations per hour, which dramatically changes team effectiveness.

ADVANCED PLAYS

Personality Data
Data providers are finally starting to unlock consistent personality data. Providers are giving guidelines on how to cold call, email, or handle meetings based on buyer personality.

It can be a great way to further optimize your outbound once you have a foundation of scalability.

Custom Signals
With enough understanding of your CRM, custom signals become an option. Website traffic, expected ad spend, ad creative, security certifications, etc. etc., are all solvable with the right tech and VAs.

The effort is a bit higher, but the payoff is incredible if done right.

Custom Personalization
With custom signals you can customize personalization as well. Use GPT integrations, custom prompts, customer quotes, etc. and you can fully customize your outbound, creating truly better results than SDRs scaled with technology.

BASE Jumps & Sales Stunts

Once my team sent drones to our closest competitor in the industry (Acme Flyer), with the message: "Apps fly higher with Beta Corp." If they agreed to a meeting, we'd then send the remote. Another competitor was called Cake, so we sent pieces of cake on dry ice to their biggest customers to entice them to switch. Right now I'm coaching a client in the private equity industry that's ingeniously sending custom poker chips in his branded color scheme with tailored value propositions to his UHNW (ultra-high net worth) prospects.

Another client sends cutting boards á la Dale Dupree with a note, "can we carve out some time?" and this strategy has an incredibly high hit rate. Check out Dale's new book and Stu Heinecke's: *How To Get a Meeting with Anyone* for ways to grab attention with cartoons and even engraved swords. (Dan Waldschmidt) I love Dale's disruptive guerrilla selling ideas like sending an eaten box of doughnuts, crumpled up letters, or printing out your email and sending it in a letter.

My record for meetings is 35 in 2 days, set at a data conference in SF by using advanced Neighborhood Technique. The classic NT is to call up a bunch of VCs in Chicago and once you set a few meetings, book the travel. I used to work the SF patch from SoCal and book a flight every two weeks. I set more face-to-face meetings than ever in my years living in the Bay in this way, because it was an event. We'd buy out a swanky restaurant and pack the private room to the gills with fine vino.

Details matter. The data conference had a hashtag on Twitter and LinkedIn. I monitored the tag and pinged every single person posting there. I simply asked for a "lobby coffee" meeting - just 5 minutes - every half hour like clockwork from 8 to 5. I booked 35 meetings and in one, my prospect brought his colleague and re-marked, "do you know who this is?" I'm like, "No." He smiled and replied, "The Founder of CareerBuilder."

Coffee in the lobby is such a low-friction ask, most prospects can't resist. A '5 min ask' works way better than carving out time in a "sitting duck" executive meeting room at a conference hall base-ment in Barcelona.

One year as a VP of Sales, I did 3MM on a 1.2MM number cover-ing only SF from LA. Every two weeks I booked a Greek dinner, Brazilian steakhouse, or conference and just neighborhooded the whole thing. Subject line: "executive meeting request" or "I'll be in town." This culminated with two dinners in LA and SF at famous Michelin star eateries packing in 30 prospects per night that gen-erated a collective 2 million in qualified pipeline.

Another couple prospecting stunts I love are FaceTime drops and Document Drops (Doc Drops). People often use Calendar Drops and that also works. All of these tactics can come with collateral damage unless you provide immediate value; the kind of value they'd pay $1,000 USD for. Here's how you do it:

- Drop into FaceTime with a laser-focused value prop
- Drop an event on the calendar with an ultra-insightful theme or famous industry speaker

- Drop a super valuable Google doc (e.g. a cheat code to unlock revenue or e-book with tactics they can apply today) - you can even drop in a deal room (like Aligned or GetAccept) that is robust to showcase many multimedia elements – docs, testimonials, videos, templates (and run reminders to it - triggered in HubSpot)
- Send an email asking if they want to see a video. It's subtle, I know - but powerful. Once they say 'yeah, send it over'- that's when I send a personalized Loom video tha's about 2 minutes long. (Hat tip Garrett Gray.) His booking rate on people that request the video has been 14%. He also suggested some new AI-based video sending platforms that take a single video and personalize it to thousands of prospects. Look into it!

It's a grey hat move to jump into people's personal digital space uninvited. WhatsApp drops are unregulated but sending an SMS without "opt-in" is technically illegal, as is a fax.

It's unlikely to be enforced, so use it wisely, probably after some interaction has happened and they know who you are; a chat flow DM on LinkedIn, or a first call. Remember the platinum rule: treat others as you know they would like to be treated.

What is a smart move and within bounds? Waterfalling prospects (hat tip Kreuzberger): this is the practice of intentionally calling someone's boss to get delegated down. Works like a charm - try it!

Here's a massive LinkedIn hack to grow your views and brand presence that's deceptively simple:

1. List the most massive profiles you're connected to with the highest follower counts.
2. Comment on their top posts (most likes and comments).

3. Leave one main *polarizing* comment (but respectful!) under that viral post and three relevant comments under other interesting responses under that thread.

It is the most overlooked guerrilla tactic to expand your LinkedIn profile overnight. Commenting 40 times a day will grow you way faster than any manner of viral attempts at posting, even carousels. Do this for 3 months, and the floodgates will open for your social media presence.

Here's a wingsuited BASE jump: consider doing *double taps*. This means calling someone's cell phone 2 or even 3 (triple tap) times in a row. But be careful, because they might think someone died or there's an emergency. You might get a bull seeing red this way. But some callers are so good tonally they can diffuse that anger. I personally don't do this one or FaceTime drops.

Is it worth the risk if you actually reach an impossible prospect live you need to talk with? Take stock of your risk profile. Again, the worst thing that can happen is "no." Despite all the threats, no one has sued me over a phone call, even after 20,000 hours of them.

One last brilliant hack I learned from Garrett MacDonald: To dramatically save time crushing my inbox, I only respond with three sentences to the highest priority messages. I tap them out on my smartphone with my thumbs and always use this signature to get away with it, which shows I'm in transit. Then I never need to write long expository messaging, which lowers read rates anyway:

<< message on the move >>

or,

<< sent from iPhone >>

In a corporate setting, where formality may be expected, it's a double upside. Field reps *should be* on the move visiting customers, so "busy" looks good. In one company where I sat on the board and advised an entire 300-person off-shore operation, I created a *3 Bullet Point Rule* for all internal managers. They'd previously written 1-2 page weekly reports, and easily 50 hours per week were wasted by senior management reading these. Instant Operations streamline hack! Productivity went through the roof. I share three genius quotes in closing this section, as you'll find they contain a silver lining of wisdom for all things JMM:

> *"Brevity is the soul of wit." – Shakespeare*

> *"Simplicity is the ultimate sophistication." – Leonardo da Vinci*

> *"I didn't have time to write a short letter, so I wrote a long one instead." – Mark Twain*

Happy BASE Jumping y'all!

CHAPTER 7: NO EXCUSES, REWRITE YOUR FUTURE

"It's always about who you need to be, not about what you need to do. What you need to do will flow from what you need to be." – Steve Chandler

Imagine it's been three years since you finished reading this book. Where are you now?

Did you take dramatic action or just let this volume collect dust on the shelf? If you applied even a fraction of everything you've read, your new "created" future should be leading you in the right direction. You should believe in your ability, and the possibility of exponential growth, and you'll no doubt be reaping the rewards.

When harnessed correctly, your attitudes will shape a customer's vision for your working relationship and the success you will achieve, merely based on your perception of them. Last but not least, to all the aspiring top sales reps out there, hold this truism dear as you flip the script:

You are scarce, and the customers are many.

Remember, the worst thing that can happen is NOT failure but not seeing your vision through to its conclusion. Dr. Wayne Dyer [RIP] said, "Don't die with your music still inside you."

Utilize the information you read in this book for the next 90 days and try to drown out any conflicting voices so that you can see how much these techniques will improve your business.

As I spread *Tech-Powered Sales* and the *Codices* around the world, the resounding feedback I received was some version of, "this is great but my manager won't let me do this. They won't pay for it. I don't have a tech stack like that. I'm blocked here."

I wrote this book to empower you wherever you are. I set records locking myself in a back room in Chinatown with just a spreadsheet, gmail, and my cell phone. My superpower? Focus. There's nothing stopping you from optimizing outbound prospecting now based on meta-frameworks, heuristics, and your understanding of the human mind.

Everything else is gravy. Icing on the cake.

Shifts come deep down in who we are being. Therefore, who we are being and how we are showing up, influences our thinking and doing.

> *"Follow your bliss and the universe will open doors where there were only walls." – Joseph Campbell*

You can take the ideas in this book anywhere, at any time, and excel. Because now you've got the understanding of trigger events and intent to pinpoint the exact 3% *in the market*. You've leveraged the extraordinary power of Pareto to unlock insurmountable "leverage" and you finally are formulating your text as C-Level decision makers actually best ingest it. From this bedrock, you can automate any aspect or leverage artificial intelligence at any point in your supply chain from targeting, to messaging, to timing.

Never forget to A/B test everything. Mastering sales is a political game to move up in organizations so being the best salesperson in your company, even industry, won't matter if your boss is a toxic energy vampire plotting to hold you down like a cog in the machine.

Repeat after me, "I am triumphantly doubling my pipeline and income with the JMM." It's that simple. People ask me, "Isn't it a bit narcissistic to call it by your name?" Sure, but Sandler did and he's changed millions of lives for the better. My answer is, "break it down, rebuild it and make it your own." e.g. The Nate Offner Method.

SERVICE-BASED PROSPECTING (SBP™) IS THE ANSWER.

Let go of trying to control everything and give that to a higher power. Chaos, in one way, is beautiful. Fractals appear everywhere in nature, and our imperfections make us truly beautiful and unique. Symmetry is a myth. That's why sales is a craft and sport - and a book can only enhance your work in the arena.

Let love into your heart and stop being so damn selfish. Abundance will flow to you and through you. You'll see. I was skeptical. Now, it's my daily walk. The curious mind turns outward. It took me 20 years to learn that, and then my income and impact exploded. It's not about you, it's about *them*. Your clients. How you can tangibly improve their lives and businesses?

Put 100% of your focus there – away from yourself. "It's not about selling; it's about helping and delivering value: sales are a byproduct and come after," paraphrasing my new friend, the luminous Charles H. Green of *Trusted Advisor*.

One of my clients left me a video, and I'll play it for you, where with tears in his eyes welling up, he explains, "By 4Xing my income, you've changed my life, Justin, and done so much for my family. I am forever grateful." I got chills, choked up a little, and was touched, teary-eyed. Why? Because this is the top of the mountain and the beginning of a new one.

My life's work is within all of you: transformation, rebirth, and ascension to your most incredible mental, physical, and spiritual heights. That's *my why*. Everything you are looking for is within you. You can find your unique genius rereading the book now from this lens, the lens of "who you are being" – hat tip, Steve Hardison. New avenues of prosperity will emerge.

> *"We are what we repeatedly do. Excellence is not an act, but a habit." – Aristotle.*

Decide today: "I will be great." I believe you will be. You are not alone or coin-operated. You matter. You are here for a reason. You can guide. You can lead. Greatness is in your DNA and birthright. Deep down, you know this is true.

Seize courage now. If you bought this book, your identity is ready to start shifting, even if it was previously dormant and waiting to be unlocked. I promise you that. I'm living proof. One insight can change your life in an instant. Ask yourself, "Do I want this bad enough?" And what is the price you'd be willing to pay – to do and be every day differently, to taste freedom and wealth at last like nectar?

We are our own worst enemy. We have to get out of our own way. That's why everything I learned from the previous 200+ coaching sessions was written down and synthesized here for your benefit: the hive mind, the mastermind – creating the movement like spinning planets.

I've only ever gone wrong when I've failed to listen to my gut instinct and inner voice. Cultivate your internal compass, and learn to trust yourself above all. Set 10X goals because they are even more accessible than incremental. They will refine your focus on the right path reducing flawed options.

Be grateful for what you are yet to receive. Gratitude will unify you with God. Commune with a higher power however you define it, and tune into the signs all around you.

Take time to find peace through silence, prayer, or meditation - being alone in nature each day away from the noise of your thoughts, feet firmly grounded in the pristine soil or sand. Come alive in the sacred solfeggio frequencies as you create what you want. It will be as you believe it, from formless moving into form in faith. Cultivate self-belief through service excellence. Soon, you will roar like a lion and unleash an unstoppable force from within.

Hindsight is always 20/20. Give, and give more. And when you're exhausted with giving, *give* even more. Trust me: Love is unlimited, an infinite game. We are on this planet to help others. Therefore, the secret to all sales is curiosity. (hat tip, Barry Rhein).

Beyond these pages, you can and will find your way to serve. Period. The end.

> *"Everybody can be great because everybody can serve," Dr. Martin Luther King Jr.*

In closing my magnum opus (and maybe you're reading this in the year 2100), I'd echo the exact, prophetic and immortal words of Albert Einstein:

> *"I have no special talent. I am only passionately curious."*

AUTHOR BIO

Justin Michael is a world-record-breaking, outbound sales maven who has arguably built the deepest client acquisition methodology of all time: the Justin Michael Method (JMM). It's driven over 1B in pipeline for 200+ startups he's advised and over 25K reps, 1K of which he's personally coached. Ex Salesforce and LinkedIn, Justin is the global authority on AI-based outbound prospecting alongside legends like Aaron Ross, Josh Braun, and Mark Roberge. His counterintuitive, mobile-responsive, neuroscience-backed visual prospecting methodology made him a million-dollar earner and helped countless startups scale past 10MM ARR. His clients frequently 2-5X their pipeline and income, consistently getting promoted within six months. Justin is the bestselling author of *Tech-Powered Sales*, which proved that over 75% of top funnel can be automated by raising your technology quotient (TQ). He lives in Los Angeles, California, advising top SaaS technology CXOs and teams on bleeding-edge GTM methods.

Also read the global #1 Bestselling book, Sales Superpowers: A New Outbound Operating System To Drive Explosive Pipeline Growth (Justin Michael Method 1.0)

Shameless plug: if you'd like 1:1 personal coaching from me on outbound customized to your scenario, you're in luck. I've co-founded the world's first ever coaching marketplace invented by Julia Nimchinski (Go here to check it out: hardskill.exchange | Ping me for a discount rate on your first session)

Learning More From Justin Michael

Find me on the web:

- **Get bonus book material at** SalesSuperpowers.com/bonus
- **Follow me on LinkedIn:** JustinMichaelMethod.com
- **GTM COMMUNITY:** Co-Founder, HYPCCCYCL. Go to HYPCCCYCL.com - #2 GTM Community in B2B (holding monthly "CXO Games" - intellectual C-Level debates) - Visit us to take the world's first GTM(A) - Assessment and benchmark your GTM expertise!
- **COACHING MARKETPLACE:** Co-Founder & CRO, Hard Skill Exchange (go to Hardskill.Exchange): World's 1st 1:1 sales coaching marketplace for practitioners. Book my coaching by the hour on-demand and become a 1% prospector. *Ping me for a discount on the first session.*
- **MASTERMINDS & TECH-POWERED REVENUE SYSTEMS:** BORG-1 at Salesborgs (go to Salesborgs.ai) - I work closely with CROs to build Superhuman Revenue Systems that are infinitely scalable and coordinate tech-powered sales mastermind groups (in WhatsApp & Discord) - Visit us to take the world's first RevTQ Test and benchmark your RevOps knowledge.
- **GTM AGENCY:** Co-Founder, N/M - Nimchinski/Michael (go to NimchinskiMichael.com) - World's first B2B go-to-market agency combining sales and marketing synergy for disruptive brand strategy, event workshops, and GTM architecture / design.

OTHER WRITINGS FEATURING JUSTIN MICHAEL:

- *Tech Powered Sales (TPS)* (TechPoweredSalesBook.com) by Justin Michael & Tony Hughes (HarperCollins)
- *Reinventing Virtual Events (RVE)* (ReinventingVirtualEvents.com) by Julia Nimchinski & Justin Michael (Wiley)
- *Codices* - hypcccycl.com/codexes/ (self-published by JM) - Log in free to download 17+ open-source prospecting guides that have driven 1B+ in pipeline
- *Combo Prospecting* (ComboProspecting.com) by Tony Hughes (HarperCollins) - JM is case study

ACKNOWLEDGEMENTS

THANK YOU:

Julia Nimchinski (GTM Inspiration), Jeremy Jones (Publishing Visionary), Tony J. Hughes (Mentor), Rebekah Carter (Editorial Lead), Nathan Finch (Editor), Greg Meyer (Technical Editor), Marco Basile (Framework Editor), Karan Korpal Sharma (GPT Whisperer), David Youngblood (GPT Whisperer), Soham Sarkar (GPT Whisperer), Scott Martinis (Tech Stack Optimization), Anthony Iannarino, Mike Weinberg, Aaron Ross, Josh Braun, Scott Britton, Max Altschuler, Lars Nilsson, Anders Fredriksson, Steve Richard, Bryan Franklin, Ben Sardella, Marcus Sandberg, Deon Don, Brendan Short, Marcus Cauchi, Jeremey Donovan, Charles Needham, Brian Q. Davis, Moeed Amin, Mark Raffan, Christian Retek, Todd Caponi, Mike Bosworth, David C. Baker, Alan Weiss, Gerry Hill, Jim Holden, Jeff Thull, Mahan Khalsa, Terry Wilson, Josh Braun, Marylou Tyler, Jed Mahrle, Luke Ruffing, Jim Thoeni, Garrett C. MacDonald, Dale Dupree, Stu Heinecke, Jim Mongillo, Colin Sutton, Dennis O'Hagan, Daniel Gray, Steve Chandler, Rich Litvin, Nathan Offner, Barrett Unger, Kellen Casebeer, Bryan Kreuzberger, Ankush Jain, Zach Selch, Victor Antonio, Townsend Wardlaw, Daniel Wax, George Foley, Frank Kohn, Doug McMillen, Nejc Škoberne, Scott Hennessy, Luke Shalom, David Hoffeld, Brian Farrell, Kevin Casey, Randy Stackaruk, Mark Baskin, Gregory

Abel, Florian Decludt, Tim Dodd, Marc Periou, Adem Manderovic, John Smibert, Steven Brady, Dario Junk, Akio Aida, Gunnar Habitz, Benjamin Dennehy, William Wacker, Mike Milewski, Miles Veth, Benjamin Misner, Mike Gallegos, Juan Pablo Garcia, Christopher Rocas, William VanSickle, Michael Koory, Pankaj Sharma, David Catalano, Peter McCammon, Kieran Krohn, Mario Krivokapic, Christian Krause, Darko Davkovski, Eric Steeves, Gavin Tice, Raj Nadar, Aditya Prakash, Joey Gilkey, Cory Bray, Moaaz Nagori, Varun Anand, Eric Nowoslawski, Lloyed Lobo, Maxence de Villepion, Charles Cormier, Patrick William Joyce.

Thank you Travis Brown, for creating the visual mindmap of JMM.